IMAGES
of America

THE SILVER BRIDGE
DISASTER OF 1967

This evocative photograph was taken soon after the Silver Bridge opened. As no other bridges existed nearby, the bridge was of tremendous social and commercial value to the region. Its opening changed the lives of everyone in the surrounding Ohio River towns. The dedication marked the largest celebration ever to take place in Point Pleasant, West Virginia. (Courtesy of Cpl. Carl Boggs family.)

ON THE COVER: The remains of this Picken's Cab Company taxi are secured aboard a recovery barge following the collapse of the Silver Bridge. A total of 31 vehicles fell with the bridge; the taxi was one of 24 that landed in the Ohio River. Both occupants in the cab were killed, along with 44 other victims. (Courtesy of the US Army Corps of Engineers.)

IMAGES
of America

THE SILVER BRIDGE
DISASTER OF 1967

Stephan G. Bullard, Bridget J. Gromek,
Martha Fout, Ruth Fout, and
the Point Pleasant River Museum

ARCADIA
PUBLISHING

Published by Arcadia Publishing
Charleston, South Carolina

Library of Congress Control Number: 2012932699

For all general information, please contact Arcadia Publishing:
Telephone 843-853-2070
Fax 843-853-0044
E-mail sales@arcadiapublishing.com
For customer service and orders:
Toll-Free 1-888-313-2665

Visit us on the Internet at www.arcadiapublishing.com

To the victims of the Silver Bridge disaster and their families

CONTENTS

ACKNOWLEDGMENTS

This book would not have been possible without the help of numerous individuals and institutions. Keith Martin, William Luecke, and Richard Fields at the National Institute of Standards and Technology helped us understand the technical aspects of the disaster. Candace Corbeil and Dennis Wasko helped with editing. Research funding was provided by Bullard and Gromek's home institution, the University of Hartford, as well as by the Joseph and Pauline Gareau Faculty Development Fund and by an Elizabeth Williams Cathles grant.

We sincerely thank many individuals and families who contributed stories or photographs for this work. We regret that space limitations prevented us from including all of the information we received. Where possible, contributors are thanked in captions.

Additional assistance was provided by Mr. and Mrs. Ray Anderson, Chris Bauer, Roger Brandenberry, Susan Brandenberry, Nancy Brown, George Byus, Tracy Call, Marianne Campbell, Walter Carpenter, Steve Chapman, Sandy Reynolds Clark, Tim Clendenen, Mary Lane Cook, Amanda Crouse, Gail Davenport, Morgan DeGraffenried, Daleen Dotson, Rhonda Sims Dixon, Brenda Taylor Fellure, Mr. and Mrs. Buddy Fowler, Don Goosman, Ann Hall, Carolyn Meadows Harris, John and Jimmy Lane, Mary Lanier, Jean Lemon, Angie Leport, Peter Lewis, Sam Matthews, Todd Mayes, Fred McCabe, Calvin McDaniel, Lew McDaniel, Debbie Darst McKinney, Donna McKinney, JoAnn McQuaid, Betty and Rhett Milhoan, Steve Moses, Willard Nibert, Virgina Oshel, Mary Boles Pearson, Genny Pickens, Marsha Powell, Mr. and Mrs. Dave Price, Buster Riffle, Robert Rimmey, Jim Ross, Jean Roush, Steve and Robert Sanders, Beth Sargent, Larry Sayre, Wanda Sanders Smith, Bertha Russell-Stover, Roxie Nibert Stover, Jeff Thompson, Robert Titus, Doris Wade, Sharon Watterson, the Paul Wedge family, Texanna White Wehrung, Janet Wetherholt, William "Slim" Willcoxen, Paul Wood, and Kristy Blazer Woodall. Special thanks goes to Jack Fowler, the director of the Point Pleasant River Museum.

Eyewitness accounts and personal stories come from interviews conducted by the authors and by the staff of the Point Pleasant River Museum; from newspaper articles from the *Point Pleasant Register*, the *Huntington Herald-Dispatch*, and the *Charleston Gazette*; and from Kristy B. Woodall's book *The Silver Bridge Disaster: The Way We Remember It*. Some information in the introduction came from CBS News and MedicineNet.com.

Many images were contributed by the Point Pleasant River Museum (PPRM) and the US Army Corps of Engineers (USACE).

INTRODUCTION

The people along the Ohio River near the town of Point Pleasant, West Virginia, had long wished for a bridge. The river was not overly wide, but reaching the opposite side was difficult and sometimes impossible. Getting across involved owning a boat, making arrangements to be ferried over, or traveling to one of the distant bridges north or south of the town.

In 1927, the region's prayers seemed to be answered when construction began on the Silver Bridge. The span was to be a modern roadway bridge connecting Point Pleasant with Kanauga, Ohio. It took two years to complete, but on May 30, 1928, the long-anticipated bridge finally opened. The joyous occasion was marked by festivities, speeches, and pageantry; everyone attended the ceremony. It was one of the most momentous events in the region's long history. Sadly—though no one in the buoyant, opening day crowd realized it—the seeds of the bridge's eventual collapse were already in place.

The Silver Bridge was intended to be an engineering marvel. It would incorporate the newest technical innovations and be of the latest design. In an era of rapidly changing technology, new ideas were constantly being integrated into construction projects. People looked forward to benefiting from these advances and were proud if their town was the first to boast a particular new type of construction. Unfortunately, some of these new ideas failed.

The Achilles heel of the Silver Bridge was its suspension system. The bridge used interlinked chains of eyebars to support the bridge deck instead of traditional cables. At the time, eyebar suspension was thought to hold several advantages over conventional designs. In practice, any advantages were greatly outweighed by the difficulty the eyebars posed to inspection and maintenance. To an inspector, a suspension chain might appear to be in perfect working order. However, because the eyebars overlapped at connection points, undetected corrosion could form on the concealed eyebar heads.

On December 15, 1967, during the height of rush hour, a corroded eyebar on the Ohio side of the river broke. This single failure caused the entire Silver Bridge to catastrophically collapse, dropping 31 vehicles and 64 people into the river and a debris pile onto the Ohio shoreline. With 46 fatalities, the fall of the Silver Bridge ranks as the worst roadway bridge collapse in US history. The exceptionally high number of casualties was a result of several factors. First, the bridge was loaded with bumper-to-bumper traffic when it fell. Second, most vehicles ended up in the frigid December waters of the Ohio River, and it took several minutes for rescue boats to arrive at the scene. Many victims never got out of their vehicles. Some of those who did escape were injured and drowned before help could reach them.

For some, bridges are always a mixed blessing. The benefit of being able to cross from one shore to another is balanced by the concerns of being high off the ground, confined within a relatively small area—inside the railings of the bridge—and being over large bodies of water. Gephyrophobia is the scientific name for the fear of crossing bridges. In some cases, this fear is so extreme that motorists drive many miles out of their way to avoid bridges. In other cases, people hire drivers to take them across particularly frightening spans, such as the Chesapeake Bay Bridge in Maryland or the Tappan Zee Bridge in New York. For many, the greatest fear is that the bridge will collapse.

Thankfully, bridge collapses are rare. Most bridges are well built, well maintained, and perfectly safe. When bridges do fall, it is usually because they have been damaged by an accident or natural disaster. Since 1900, a total of 19 major roadway bridges have collapsed in the United States. About half of these fell because ships collided with them or because major traffic accidents occurred on them. Bridges have also fallen because of river scour, shifting riverbeds, ice collisions, and earthquakes. Only five bridges, including the Silver Bridge, have collapsed because of poor design or improper maintenance.

One of the better-known bridge collapses was the fall of the Tacoma Narrows Bridge, which crossed a portion of the Puget Sound in Washington State, in November 1940. The bridge was not well designed for its location, and high winds caused the bridge deck to buckle dramatically. On November 7, the bridge's amazing oscillations—at the time, the deck was bending up to 28 feet high—and catastrophic collapse were captured by film crews. Fortunately, no one was killed.

More recently, in August 2007, the I-35W Mississippi River Bridge in Minneapolis, Minnesota, collapsed due to a design error. Like the Silver Bridge, the Minneapolis Bridge fell during rush hour. At the time, 111 vehicles were on the bridge and 13 people died. The direct cause of this collapse was the presence of undersized gusset plates coupled with an increase in bridge weight from roadway upgrades. Gusset plates are steel plates used to connect beams and girders to columns. Because the gusset plates used in the I-35W Mississippi River Bridge were too small, they could not support the increased weight of the bridge.

The collapse of the Silver Bridge was a watershed moment for US civil engineering and for the oversight and maintenance of highway infrastructure. As a direct result of the collapse, a nationwide inspection of bridges was undertaken. Many were found to be in dangerous condition and in desperate need of maintenance. The widespread repairs brought about by the fall of the Silver Bridge almost certainly prevented additional collapses. As a long-term engineering legacy, modern bridge construction now devotes additional attention to the soundness and safety of support and truss design.

These reforms are the silver lining of the Silver Bridge disaster. While its collapse tragically ended the lives of many innocent victims, it also led to critical safety reforms that have undoubtedly saved the lives of many others.

One

CONSTRUCTION AND
LIFE OF THE BRIDGE

For the small communities along the Ohio River near Point Pleasant, West Virginia, 1928 was a watershed year. Before that time, the two sides of the river were largely isolated and the only way to get across was by ferry. Although some people crossed on a regular basis and many crossed occasionally, going back and forth between Ohio and West Virginia was generally a rare event. That changed with the opening of the Silver Bridge. Overnight, the towns of Point Pleasant and Kanauga and Gallipolis, Ohio, became connected in a direct and meaningful way.

With this new connectivity came new opportunities. People could now work and shop on either side of the river. Visitors also became a major part of the community. Historically, the region had been more or less cut off from the outside world. After 1928, travelers passed through on a regular basis. While in the area, visitors needed food, gas, entertainment, and sometimes a place to stay. As a result, the opening of the Silver Bridge sparked significant development in the surrounding towns. For almost 40 years, the bridge successfully fulfilled its job of transporting people across the river.

When constructed, the Silver Bridge was intended to be a vital, architecturally interesting yet relatively unremarkable roadway structure. Its job was to connect several small towns on the Ohio River and provide a direct link between Columbus, Ohio, and Charleston, West Virginia. Had it not catastrophically collapsed, the Silver Bridge would have most likely lived out its useful life like most bridges. It would be heavily used by travelers but would quickly fade from memory as people crossed it and continued on their journeys. This was not to be, however. At dusk on December 15, 1967, the bridge collapsed, carrying 46 people to their deaths. Instead of standing in relative anonymity, the name of the Silver Bridge became etched into the historical record. This photograph captures the majesty of the bridge in its prime. The bright silver structure seems to soar above the river and dominates the skyline. (Courtesy of Carolyn Costen Hartenbach.)

Sometimes called the father of the Silver Bridge, Dr. Charles Holzer Sr. leans against the pedestrian guardrail of the bridge soon after its dedication. Dr. Holzer was a cornerstone of the river communities and a beloved local patron. In the 1910s, he was the only surgeon in the tri-county area and worked on both sides of the Ohio River. Transportation across the river was often hard to find, especially at odd hours of the day and in bad weather. Some patients died waiting for help simply because the doctor could not reach them in time. After a particularly dangerous winter crossing, Dr. Holzer decided that action needed to be taken. Enlisting the help of several well-positioned friends, Dr. Holzer formed the Mason County Bridge Company to begin the task of building a bridge. Ironically, many of the victims of the 1967 collapse would be treated in Dr. Holzer's namesake, Holzer Hospital. (Courtesy of Mrs. Charles "Bobby" Holzer Jr.)

The formation of the Mason County Bridge Company was only the first step towards the construction of the Silver Bridge. A sister enterprise, the Gallipolis County Bridge Company, also spearheaded by Dr. Holzer, was organized on the Ohio side of the river. Later, these organizations merged into the Gallia County Ohio River Bridge Company, which received permission to build the bridge on May 13, 1926. Construction was undertaken by the West Virginia-Ohio River Bridge Corporation and the American Bridge Company. Though company names changed over time, many of the same people remained involved with the project. Here, the bridge is seen midway though construction. It was built more or less from the top down, with its towers constructed first, followed by the suspension chains. Finally, the bridge deck was laid. Photographs of the bridge before the decking was added are rare. (Courtesy of Patty Carman.)

The photograph at right shows the bridge construction at a more advanced stage. Workmen are busy laying the foundation for the bridge deck. Of interest is the rudimentary safety equipment provided for the workers. The safety conditions exhibited in this photograph are vastly different than those found at a modern construction site. (Courtesy of PPRM.)

Below, some of the workmen who built the Silver Bridge take a break to pose for a photograph when construction was nearly complete. Only the roadway asphalt remained to be laid. (Courtesy of PPRM.)

THE MILLION DOLLAR GALLIPOLIS PT. PLEASANT BRIDGE

THE Gallipolis-Point Pleasant "Silver Bridge" is so new in its engineering conception that it is attracting world-wide attention. It is a two-way vehicular bridge of the suspension type, but instead of the usual woven-wire cable, the bridge is suspended on heat-treated eye-bar chains. It is the first bridge in America of this design and the second in the world. The quality of steel used in the eye-bar chains is of the very highest. It has a tensile strength of 150,000 pounds per square inch, which allows a safe stress far in excess of ordinary structural steel.

The total length of the bridge is 2235 feet. On either side approaching the suspended spans is a 200' anchorage and a steel-plate, deck-girder span 148' 9" long. The suspended structure consists of two side spans 380' long, and the main channel span 700' long and 102' above zero gauge or low water in the Ohio River. The bridge has a roadway 22' wide and a 5' 6" sidewalk. This bridge was built in less than one year from the time work started upon it,—a record for the designer and builder.

This is the first bridge in the world to be painted with aluminum paint. The silver-like effect of this paint, flashing from the steel work of the bridge, is responsible for its unique name. It will be illuminated at night by flood lights specially designed for it, which throw it into bright relief against the darkness.

Total cost of the bridge was $1,200,000.

The WEST VIRGINIA OHIO RIVER BRIDGE CO.
OWNERS

Incorporated under the laws of Delaware

DR. CHARLES E. HOLZER, Gallipolis, O.	President
WALTER A. WINDSOR, Point Pleasant, W. Va.	Sec'y-Treas.
MCLAUGHLIN, MCAFEE & Co., Pittsburgh, Pa.	Bankers
MACKUBIN, GOODRICH & Co., Baltimore, Md.	Bankers
THE J. E. GREINER Co., Baltimore	Designing Engineers
PROF. CLYDE T. MORRIS, head of the Department of Engineering, Ohio State University	Consulting Engineer
GENERAL CONTRACTING Co., Pittsburgh	Contractors
AMERICAN BRIDGE Co., Pittsburgh	Steel Construction

This page, highlighting the bridge's attributes, comes from a pamphlet produced for the dedication of the Silver Bridge. Considerable attention is drawn to the bridge's innovative design. The bridge was an eyebar suspension bridge designed by the J.E. Greiner Company. It differed from traditional suspension bridges in that it used a series of interlocking steel eyebars to support the bridge deck instead of wire cables. At the time, only one other bridge in the world, the Florianopolis Bridge in Brazil, was built using these techniques. Soon a third—and the last of similar style—eyebar suspension bridge would be built at St. Mary's, West Virginia, about 90 miles north of Point Pleasant. The pamphlet also highlights the aluminum paint that covered the bridge. The silvery paint gave the Silver Bridge its name and unique character. (Courtesy of Robert Keathley.)

The Silver Bridge.

COPYRIGHT 1928
F. J. Luckwell.

The bridge was built in 1927–1928 and opened officially on May 30, 1928. While different sources list different costs for the bridge, most cite a figure of $1.2 million. However, a 1928 financial statement by the American Bridge Company states that the cost was $900,000. The Silver Bridge was operated as a toll bridge by the West Virginia-Ohio River Bridge Corporation with a single tollbooth present on the Ohio side of the river. Many of the bridge's structural features, including the tollbooth, are seen here. Very little development is apparent on the West Virginia side at the time. Over the years, the skyline of Point Pleasant has changed significantly. The town has expanded northward, and many large buildings have been constructed. Recent riverfront renovations have also changed the look of the West Virginia shoreline. (Courtesy of William Emory Monroe.)

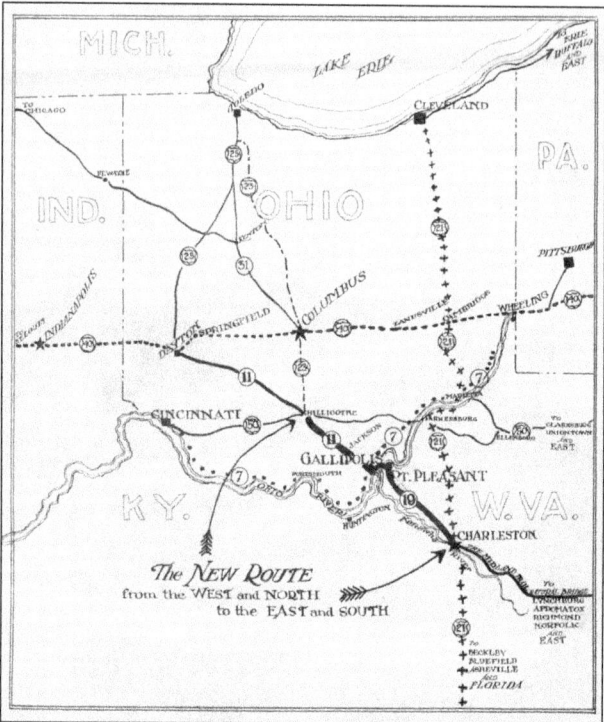

Another name for the Silver Bridge was the "Gateway to the South." Before the bridge was opened, no direct path connected the commercially important cities of Columbus, Ohio, and Charleston, West Virginia. The Silver Bridge changed that and helped connect the region with the outside world. (Courtesy of Robert Keathley.)

The aerial view below—taken sometime after 1950, as indicated by the greater development and the presence of the flood wall— illustrates the local importance of the Silver Bridge. The next closest bridges were 41 miles south at Huntington, West Virginia, and 14 miles north at Mason, West Virginia. (Courtesy of USACE.)

On May 30, 1928, the Silver Bridge was dedicated and officially opened to traffic. This was a momentous occasion for the surrounding communities. At last crossing the river would be a simple matter. No longer would travel be dictated by the weather or the need to wait for a ferry. Dignitaries, public figures, and local people flocked to the celebration. The governor of West Virginia, congressmen from West Virginia and Ohio, and a West Virginia senator made opening remarks. Crowds were even treated to an airplane squadron flyby, a rare event at the time. These are the cover and interior pages from the program for the dedication ceremonies. (Both, courtesy of Donna Brinker.)

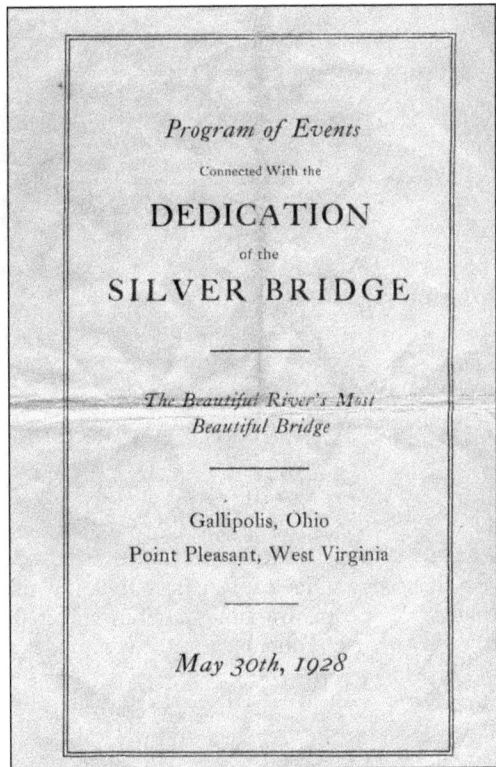

Program of Events

Connected With the

DEDICATION

of the

SILVER BRIDGE

The Beautiful River's Most Beautiful Bridge

Gallipolis, Ohio

Point Pleasant, West Virginia

May 30th, 1928

Automobile Parade

12:30 p.m. Decorated automobiles assemble in Point Pleasant in lines designated by American Legion Police.
Parade starts at 1:00 p.m., preceded by heralds on horseback and the Beni-Kedem Shrine Band.
Line of parade across the Silver Bridge down through Gallipolis and return to scene of dedication. Judges will be stationed on the bridge and will select the best decorated cars of Ohio and West Virginia for prizes.

Speaking Program

2:00 p.m. Introduction—Judge R. J. Mauck, of Ohio, Master of Ceremonies.

2:10 p.m. Governor Howard M. Gore, of West Virginia.

2:20 p.m. Lieutenant-Governor William G. Pickrel, of Ohio.

2:30 p.m. Congressman James A. Hughes, of West Virginia.

2:35 p.m. Congressman Thomas A. Jenkins, of Ohio.

2:40 p.m. Presentation of the bridge officials, bankers and builders.

3:00 p.m. Address of the day—Senator Mansfield M. Neely, of West Virginia.

3:30 p.m. Presentation of the ferry franchise—Captain W. E. McDade.

3:40 p.m. Conferring of prizes won in the automobile parade.

Pageant

3:45 p.m. Long roll of drums.
The pageant will take place on the deck girder span of the bridge in full view of the crowd assembled in the field below. A procession representing historical characters and events will pass before the audience as the interpreter reads his discourse on the "REALIZATION OF A DREAM."

Dedication of the Bridge

As the curtain is drawn aside it reveals behind a ribbon barrier, Miss Point Pleasant, a colonial belle, and her attendants. From the Ohio side approaches a young French gallant representing Gallipolis, Ancient City of the Gaul. He greets her across the barrier and they stand there while officials of both states meet and shake hands across the ribbon.

Christening of the Bridge

Miss Elizabeth Ann Holzer   Miss Ann Park Windsor

After the christening of the Silver Bridge Miss Point Pleasant and Mr. Gallipolis will untie the ribbon barrier and open the bridge to the public. Miss Point Pleasant with her attendants, and Mr. Gallipolis will enter an awaiting car. With them will be the little girls, christeners of the bridge. They will head the celebration parade.

Behind them will come the participants in the pageant, the speakers and officials on foot, the Beni-Kedem Shrine Band, and all the automobiles of the crowds attending. The bridge will be open until the fireworks program in the evening.

Airplane Squadron

A squadron of airplanes will fly over the scene, and following the bridge dedication a double parachute drop will be made from two planes 3000 feet above the river.

Fireworks Program

8:15 p.m. This will be a gorgeous pyrotechnic display of half an hour.

Grand Ball

9:00 p.m. A dance will be held at Recreation Hall of the Ohio Hospital for Epileptics, Gallipolis. Admission will be by card.

This image is a frame capture from the only surviving movie of the dedication ceremonies. More than 10,000 people are thought to have taken part in the celebration, making it the largest crowd to ever gather in Point Pleasant. Even modern events do not draw as many visitors. (Courtesy of PPRM.)

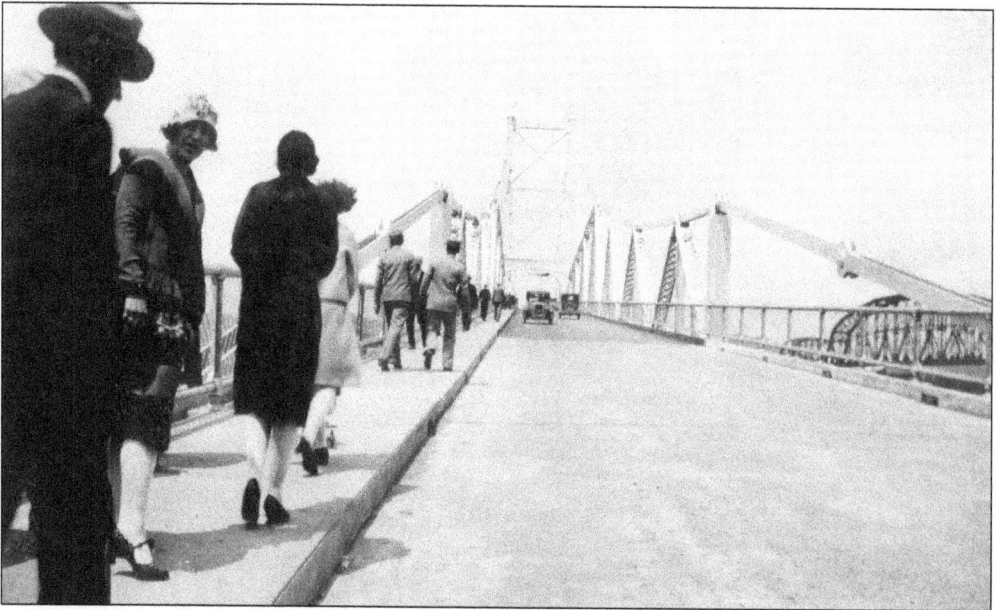

It is not an overstatement to say that the opening of the Silver Bridge changed the lives of everyone in the area. Here, some of the first cars and pedestrians cross the bridge. One can almost feel the excitement and pride of the visitors as they look down at the river from the height of the bridge. (Courtesy of Charles Garland.)

OHIO
RIVER

FERRY
LANDING
OLD

GREAT KANAWHA
RIVER

Pt. PLEASANT W.VA
July 30. 1931.

BOLLINGER. PHOTO.
HUNTINGTON +
CHARLESTON
W.VA

After its dedication, the Silver Bridge began its life as a pivotal local roadway. This fantastic aerial view looks towards the northeast and shows the important geographical features surrounding the bridge. The state of West Virginia is to the east (right), and Ohio is to the west (left). Due to its light color, the Silver Bridge is somewhat hard to see at the left center of the photograph; the adjacent railroad bridge stands out with more contrast. The town of Point Pleasant occupies the east bank of the Ohio River with its commercial center filling the rectangular area framed by the three bridges. Close observation reveals some prominent town structures, such as the Lowe Hotel. The cluster of buildings south of the bridge on the Ohio side of the river is the village of Kanauga. Gallipolis, Ohio, is off camera to the south. (Courtesy of PPRM.)

This photograph is labeled May 30, 1928, the day of the bridge dedication, but it may have been taken a few days before or after the ceremonies. The short, eastward leaning shadows indicate that the picture was taken in the mid-afternoon. Yet the bridge appears deserted, and there is no sign of the massive crowds. The sky is overcast, however, and a rain shower did interrupt the

opening parade. The photograph nicely illustrates Kanauga, Ohio, and the bridge approach from the Ohio side. As a panoramic view, it also better illustrates the size of the Silver Bridge than traditionally formatted photographs. (Courtesy of Jim Roach family.)

General Lafayette was entertained in this old tavern which is now open to the public as a museum.

OUR HOUSE-GALLIPOLIS, OHIO.

The first battle of the American Revolution was fought at this point.

POINT PLEASANT, WVA.

We crossed the Ohio River over the Million Dollar SILVER BRIDGE, the most beautiful bridge in the United States, and first of its type of construction. The shortest route from North and West to the Atlantic Seaboard with perfect highways.

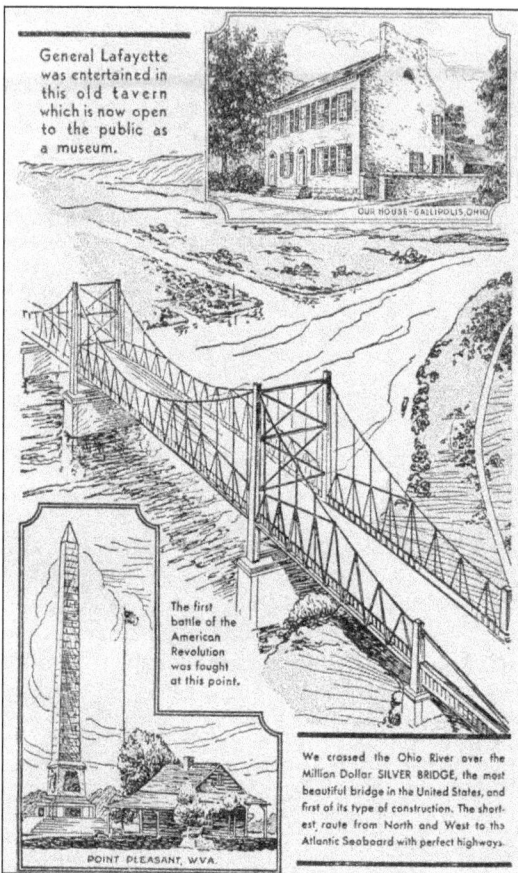

The pride the local communities felt towards the Silver Bridge can be seen in these postcards. Many small towns created similar postcards to document important local buildings and events. In the illustration at left, the Silver Bridge takes a central place in a grouping of area historical sites. The bridge's attractive design and regional importance are highlighted by the accompanying text. The postcard below looks across the bridge from the West Virginia side of the river. On the original, the scene is attractively colored with the bridge arch beckoning seductively across blue waters toward distant green hills. (Both, courtesy of Stephan Bullard.)

Silver Bridge and New York Central Bridge across Ohio River

Connecting Point Pleasant, W. Va. and Gallipolis, Ohio

ZA544-N

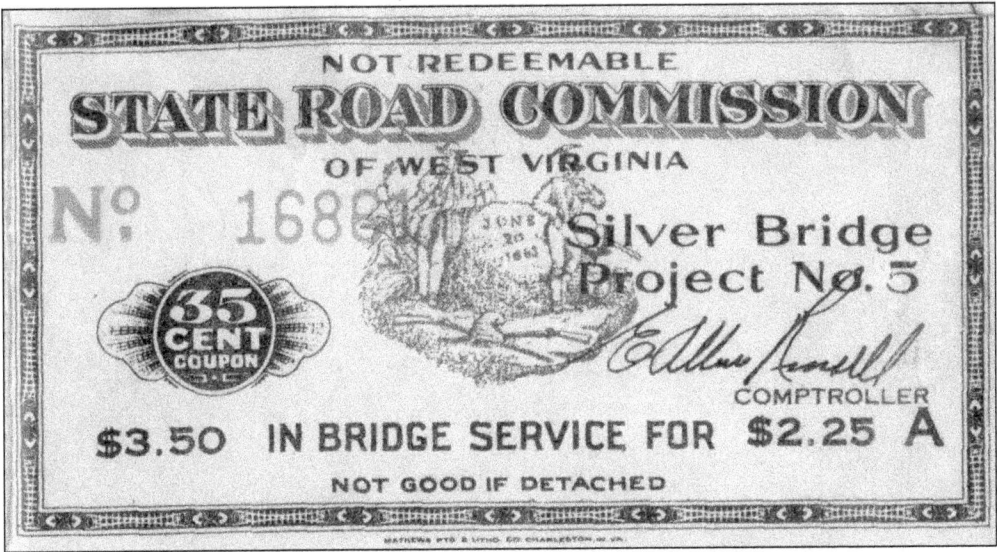

NOT REDEEMABLE

STATE ROAD COMMISSION

OF WEST VIRGINIA

Nọ 1686 ... Silver Bridge Project Nọ. 5

35 CENT COUPON

COMPTROLLER

$3.50 IN BRIDGE SERVICE FOR $2.25 A

NOT GOOD IF DETACHED

Shown here are two versions of Silver Bridge toll tickets. Ticket designs and prices varied over the life of the bridge. Individual tickets could be purchased at the bridge, or frequent users could buy ticket booklets in advance. There were different toll rates for vehicles and pedestrians. For a time, vehicle passes cost 35¢ each, but booklets of 10 could be purchased for $2.25 (above). Early pedestrian tickets featured Dr. Holzer's signature (below). Many surviving toll tickets are kept as family relics and as mementos of the Silver Bridge. (Above, courtesy of Robert Keathley; below, courtesy of Point Pleasant Presbyterian Church.)

The West Virginia-Ohio River Bridge Company

Foot Passenger Ticket Good for One Crossing

Charles E. Holzer

PRESIDENT

A321739

One of the most significant problems faced by communities along the Ohio River is the danger of flooding. Floods occurred frequently during the life of the bridge, with some of the most serious events happening in 1913, 1933, 1937, and 1948. At times, large sections of Point Pleasant were submerged. In the above image, Henderson, West Virginia (foreground), and Kanauga, Ohio, are both under water. Below, downtown Point Pleasant and the approach to the Silver Bridge are inundated. (Above, courtesy of Robert Keathley; below, courtesy of Charles Towner.)

In this amazing photograph, a young man uses a small boat to navigate Main Street in Point Pleasant during a flood. The West Virginia bridge approach, with a car parked on the ramp to avoid the floodwaters, is in the background. "March 1936" was written on the back of the original photograph, but this image may have been taken during the 1937 flood. (Courtesy of Charles Towner.)

To deal with the flood hazard, Point Pleasant began erecting a flood wall in 1949, seen here as it nears completion in December 1950. The Point Pleasant River Museum currently occupies the large white building just behind the wall in the center. In the distance, the Silver Bridge stands against the skyline. (Courtesy of Robert Keathley and USACE.)

Ice and snow were another common problem around the bridge. Winters in the region are often severe; during the coldest periods, thick ice can form on the Ohio River (above). In modern times, this problem has been largely solved by the building of the Gallipolis Locks and Dam. The river has not frozen solid since these were constructed. Fresh snow covers the West Virginia Silver Bridge approach (below) and traffic does not seem to be moving—no tire tracks are present on the bridge or on the streets in the foreground. (Above, courtesy of William Emory Monroe; below, courtesy of John Franklin.)

Both of these photographs were taken during the winter of 1948. The river has frozen, and six or eight inches of snow cover the ice. The Silver Bridge looks especially regal against the light-colored background in the above image. Below, a group of Point Pleasant locals have cleared a small spot for ice-skating. This was a welcome activity for cooped-up youngsters at a time when less entertainment was available at home. Tracks in the distance suggest that at least one person has crossed the river on the ice. (Both, courtesy of Paula Taylor.)

In 1941, when America was entering World War II, the Silver Bridge underwent extensive renovations. The roadway, originally made of wood planks covered with asphalt, was replaced by a concrete-filled steel grid. The road was also widened. This photograph is of the initial bridge construction in 1928. (Courtesy of PPRM.)

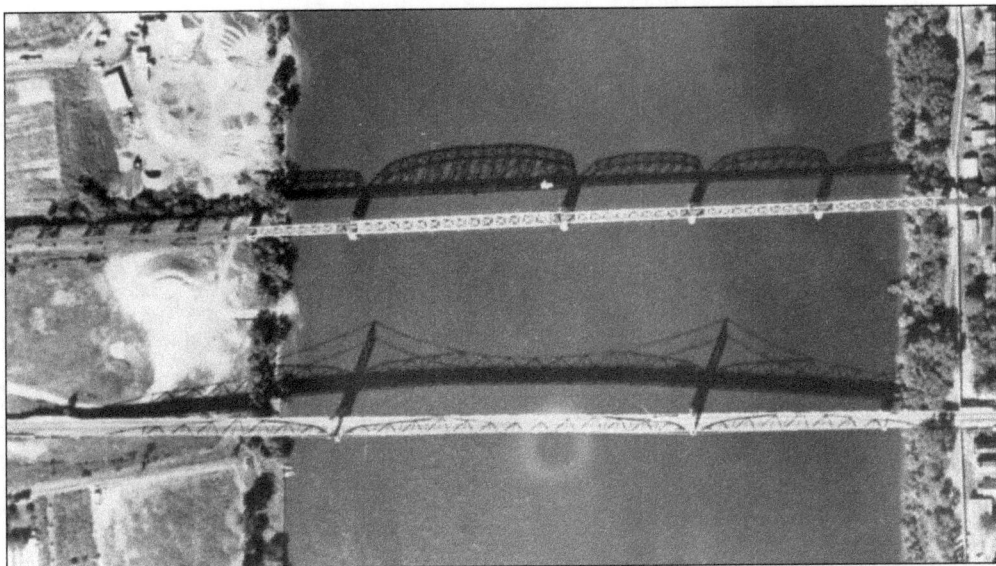

Through the nastiest weather and supporting the heaviest loads, the Silver Bridge dutifully served the local communities for almost 40 years. It became so enmeshed with the local consciousness that few could think of Point Pleasant without thinking about the bridge. By 1967, many local people had seen the bridge on the skyline for their entire lives. These two photographs illustrate the Silver Bridge during its working life. The remarkable aerial view above examines the bridge from almost directly overhead. The bridge's distinctive outline is visible as a shadow. Below, an oblique aerial view looks towards Point Pleasant and the relatively undeveloped land beyond it. (Both, courtesy of USACE.)

To those who lived and worked along the Ohio River, the Silver Bridge seemed like part of the family. It was a trusted companion they traveled across frequently, sometimes several times a day. True, some people said that the bridge had a tendency to sway and, like all large bridges, some were uncomfortable crossing it. The majority of people, however, gave it little thought. When they did think about the bridge, they tended to do so with pride. As for the swaying, those in the know attributed any movement to the innovated rocker construction of the bridge towers. The towers were somewhat flexible and could move with the suspension chains to help reduce strain on the bridge piers. Almost everyone in the area trusted the Silver Bridge and expected it to be with them long into the future. (Courtesy of USACE.)

Two

COLLAPSE OF THE
SILVER BRIDGE

At 4:58 p.m. on Friday, December 15, 1967, the Silver Bridge suddenly and unexpectedly collapsed. Disasters, by their very nature, are unanticipated. But it cannot be overstated how unexpected the collapse was. To think that such an integral part of the local backdrop could give way was unimaginable.

The effects of the collapse were devastating. It occurred at perhaps the worst possible moment: during the height of rush hour, when the bridge was loaded with commuters and early Christmas shoppers. A total of 38 vehicles were on the bridge at the time. Of these, 31 fell into the river or became enmeshed in a debris pile on the Ohio shoreline. The other seven were on the bridge approaches and did not fall. In all, 64 people fell with the bridge, 46 of whom were killed. Each victim faced their own personal hell during the disaster. About 80 percent of those who died drowned. The others died from severe trauma. Two victims disappeared into the river and were never recovered. This chapter focuses on the collapse and its immediate aftermath. When possible, events are described through first-person eyewitnesses and survivor accounts.

The collapse began when one of the eyebars on the northern side of the bridge, near the Ohio side of the river, broke. The eyebar suspension chains held the bridge deck up. When one chain broke, the weight of the bridge was no longer supported, and in rapid succession, the chains, towers, and bridge deck all collapsed. An observer watching from the shoreline would have seen the bridge start to fall on the Ohio side followed by a wave of destruction spreading rapidly towards the West Virginia side. It took about one minute for the Silver Bridge to completely collapse, and most people had little or no warning that the bridge was falling. A few, especially those near the West Virginia side, had several moments to react. At least one, Charlene Wood, on the West Virginia approach, was able to take evasive action. (Courtesy of PPRM.)

This was the scene that greeted survivors, rescue workers, and relatives on the night of December 15, 1967. All that remained of the Silver Bridge was a twisted heap of metal and fallen cars. The bridge collapsed at 4:58 p.m., and with sunset around 5:07 p.m., darkness came quickly. Initially, rescuers used car headlights and flashlights to illuminate the scene. Later, workers brought floodlights, some of which are seen here attached to trees and elevated pieces of wreckage. Emergency crews worked in an eerie and treacherous landscape and were forced to negotiate jagged, unstable debris to reach survivors. (Both, courtesy of the *Herald-Dispatch*.)

In the days following the collapse, Ohio state trooper Cpl. Carl Boggs assisted on both sides of the river and took a remarkable series of photographs. These photographs, all labeled "Courtesy of Cpl. Carl Boggs family," provide a comprehensive tour of the disaster site. These two photographs show the northern side of the bridge on the Ohio side. In the above image, a trooper, just left of center, helps direct traffic through the area. Below, tow trucks struggle to remove wreckage while the parked cars of rescue workers fill the foreground. (Both, courtesy of Cpl. Carl Boggs family.)

This panoramic view was taken from the top of the surviving portion of the Ohio bridge approach—where the people are standing in the photograph at the top of the following page. It graphically illustrates the conditions of the disaster site. Four vehicles are visible in the rubble. Closest to the camera is Paul Hayman's red and black Pontiac. Next are the remains of the McLean Trucking Company's truck. Beyond, on its passenger side on the top of the debris pile, is the Cantrell's station wagon. Finally, Gerald McManus's pickup truck faces the camera near the riverbank. Three of the eight people in these vehicles died: Melvin Cantrell and Cecil Counts in the station wagon and Gerald McManus in the pickup. Running from right to left across the photograph are the remains of the southern eyebar chain. (Courtesy of Cpl. Carl Boggs family.)

Fragments of the bridge deck and a large section of the southern eyebar chain lie in front of the Ohio side of the bridge approach. This photograph was taken very close to the spot where the critical eyebar, number 330, failed. Eyebar 330 was located directly above and perhaps 20 yards to the rear of this location. (Courtesy of Cpl. Carl Boggs family.)

Jeff Thompson, seven years old at the time, was playing football in the backyard of his house on Viand Street in Point Pleasant when he saw the bridge fall. "I remember the bridge swaying first one way, and then back the other, before finally settling in the middle again, and then, it just dropped out of the sky," he recalls. (Courtesy of PPRM.)

Victims on the bridge had a horrifying front-row seat to the collapse. Paul A. Scott, in James Pullen's 1965 Dodge, was at almost the exact center of the bridge. He recalls that just before the collapse, "It seemed to me that the bridge was shaking sideways—the automobile seemed like it was shaking sideways five or six inches." (Courtesy of Cpl. Carl Boggs family.)

Other survivors had different experiences. Howard Boggs remembers the bridge going very quickly. "It started to shake up and down, and that was it." Frank Wamsley did not feel the shaking. "The first thing I noticed was that the bridge was leaning to the right and just rolling." (Courtesy of Cpl. Carl Boggs family.)

For those who fell with the bridge, the actual collapse was only part of the horror. Some cars landed in a debris pile on the Ohio shoreline (above). Margaret Cantrell was in her station wagon (below) with her husband, Melvin Cantrell, and friend Cecil Counts. Once the terrible noise of the collapse subsided, a deep, oppressive silence set in. For the rest of her life, Margaret Cantrell always had to have a radio or television on because too much quiet reminded her of the horrible silence she experienced after the fall of the Silver Bridge. (Above, courtesy of Darlene Haer; below, courtesy of Cpl. Carl Boggs family.)

Many vehicles ended up in the river. People in these not only had to deal with the trauma of the collapse, but also with the deadly risk posed by the Ohio River. William "Bill" Needham (above) was in a Roadway Express truck near the center of the bridge. The following is a slightly abbreviated account of his story as published in the *Point Pleasant Register*: "We hit the water and the truck sank like a rock. I found one window a half to three-quarters down. That's how I escaped. I didn't know how far I had to go up. But I could tell the water kept getting lighter. When I got to the top my back hurt and I reached for a box floating by. I couldn't move my feet so I paddled with my hands . . . then hollered for help. The boat [belonging to City Ice and Fuel] picked me up about 15 minutes later." This photograph shows Needham in 1977. (Courtesy of Bill Needham.)

Ronald Sims and Bobby Head were riding in this white Pontiac Firebird when the bridge collapsed. This photograph, taken several months before the disaster, shows Sims's twin daughters, Ronda (left) and Tammy, standing in front of the car. Sims was a skilled amateur mechanic and spent a great deal of time tinkering with his beloved Firebird. (Courtesy of Kay Sims Quimby.)

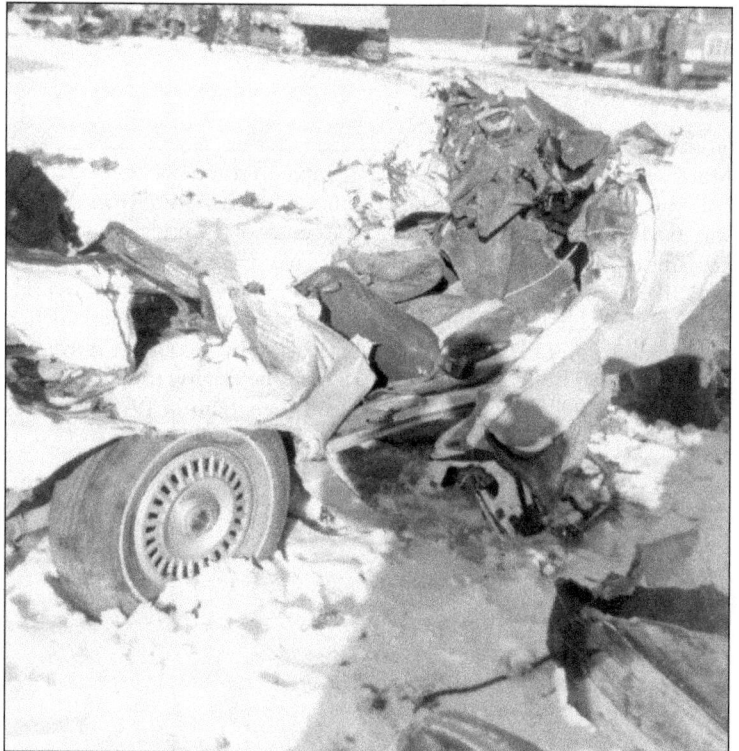

These are the remains of the Firebird after the disaster. This photograph was taken from the rear of the passenger side looking towards the driver's seat. Ronald Sims and Bobby Head were both killed, and their bodies were recovered outside the vehicle. Head's wedding ring was found inside the car. (Courtesy of Kay Sims Quimby.)

Witnesses on shore could only watch as victims struggled in the water. Ronald Dale Roush was waiting at an intersection in Point Pleasant when he heard the bridge fall. He wrote the following account on the day of the disaster. "The bridge had fallen! I kept looking at the missing structure which had just stood a second ago. I ran up the bridge's approach. There I witnessed the agony of death as a passenger in one automobile tried to break the glass in his car, which was sinking quickly to the bottom of the river." Others saw victims floating on objects and calling for help. (Above, courtesy of Cpl. Carl Boggs family; below, courtesy of Kay Sims Quimby.)

Many people had close calls with the bridge. Jim McLaughlin was an overland truck driver on his way from Akron, Ohio, to Charlotte, North Carolina. He was friends with Bob Evans and normally stopped at Bob Evans Restaurant in Gallipolis. On this day, he was in a hurry, so Evans simply gave him a cup of coffee and McLaughlin got back on the road. As he was crossing the bridge, the coffee unexpectedly slipped off the dashboard. A few minutes later, he stopped for fuel on Route 35. When he went inside to pay, he was told that the bridge had just fallen. He still wonders if it was the swaying of the bridge at the start of the collapse that caused his coffee to spill. (Both, courtesy of PPRM.)

Peggy Huber lived in Gallipolis, Ohio. The night of the collapse, her father asked her to go to Point Pleasant to pick up a ring for him. She crossed the bridge in her new Camaro convertible (above). Finishing her errand, she tried to get back on the road, but heavy traffic kept her from immediately leaving the parking lot. When she finally got moving, she was caught by the red light at the bottom of the West Virginia bridge approach (below). As she waited for the light, she "heard such an awful sound of metal falling. I looked up and saw what remained of a huge bridge fall like a tinker toy into the water." Huber missed being on the bridge because of a few trivial delays. (Above, courtesy of Peggy Huber; below, courtesy of Cpl. Carl Boggs family.)

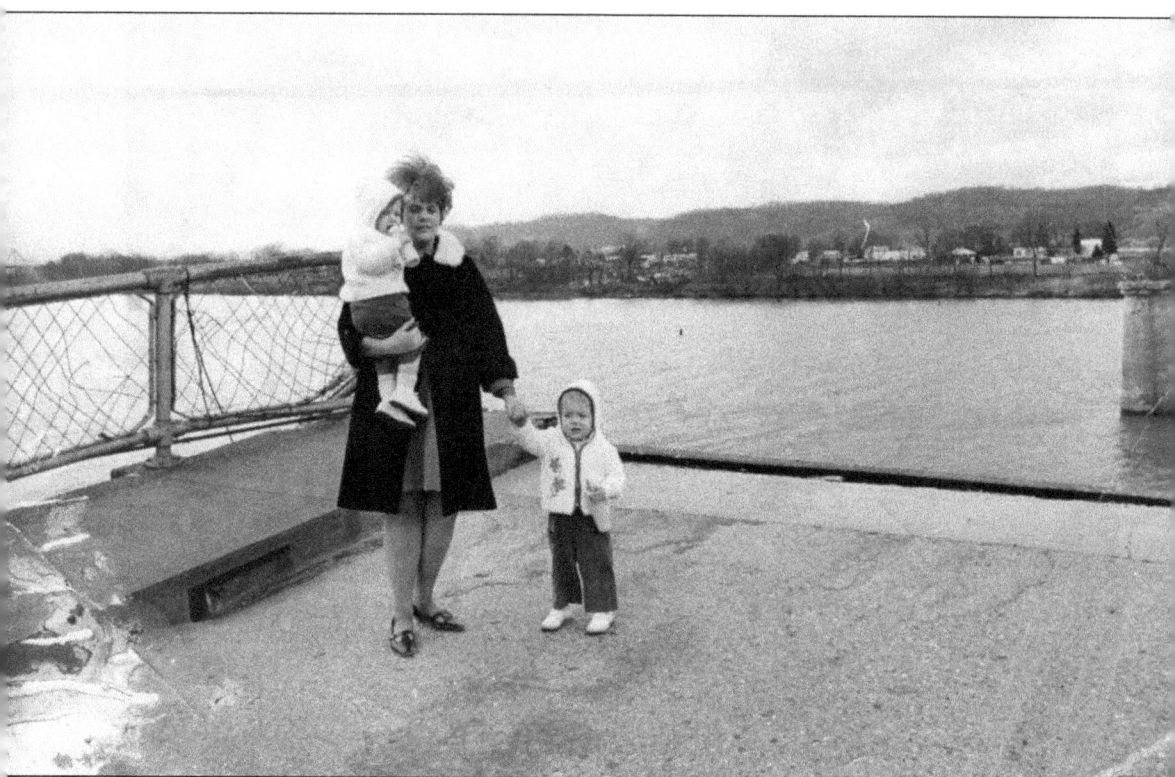

Perhaps no one had a closer call than Charlene Wood, who was five months pregnant with twins at the time of the disaster. She had just started up the West Virginia approach when the bridge began to fall. She recalls: "I felt a shaking of the bridge. I wasn't going across so I threw my car in reverse. The shaking was so severe my car died, but it kept rolling back because of the incline. As I was watching in horror, the bridge was falling right in front of my eyes. It was like someone had lined up dominos in a row, and gave them a push, and they all came falling down and there was a great big splash of water. I could see car lights flashing as they were tumbling into the water. The car in front of me went in. Then there was silence." This photograph shows Charlene and her twins returning to the edge of the approach where her car had stopped. (Courtesy of Carlos Wood family.)

As soon as the bridge was down, people raced to help survivors. Frank Shoemaker, who operated a Christmas tree lot near the bridge on the Ohio side of the river, was one of the first to reach the scene. "There were people screaming and cars and trucks upside down, on their sides and every which way," he recalls. "I saw two trucks really mangled." (Courtesy of Cpl. Carl Boggs family.)

Shoemaker continues, "There was a black car, I don't know what make, with a gentleman hanging out the window. He said he was alive and there was someone under him alive too, because he could feel them breathing. There had been a third person in the car but we couldn't see anyone else." (Courtesy of Cpl. Carl Boggs family.)

Bill McCormick was at the City Ice and Fuel landing—seen here with the boat before the disaster—when he saw the bridge fall. He and another man jumped into the City Ice and Fuel boat and headed to the scene. He recalls "people were hanging on to flotsam from the tractor-trailers that had been on the bridge. The last person rescued, a captain from the Ohio River Company, said he couldn't have held on much longer." Together, they managed to pull four men from the river. At the time of the collapse, the water temperature was 44 degrees. At these temperatures, an exposed person will rapidly become exhausted and lose consciousness. In all, only five survivors were pulled from the river. (Above, courtesy of Butch Brinker; below, courtesy of Jim Roach family.)

The injured were transported to local hospitals as quickly as possible. Bertha Russell-Stover worked in the emergency room of Holzer Hospital in Gallipolis, Ohio (above). She recalls, "When the call came, the operator said that the Silver Bridge had collapsed and to get ready for an overwhelming amount of injuries. Not believing this, all were shocked when ambulances started arriving with injured and dead people. The nurses scrambled to get toe tags for the living and the dead as so many people did not have an ID. Someone was stationed at the entrance to the ER declaring those dead, and a temporary morgue was set up at Grace Methodist Church" (below). (Above, courtesy of David Tawney, Tawney's Studio; below, courtesy of Mary Niday.)

Victims were also taken to Pleasant Valley Hospital, where office manager Margaret Amburgey received a call about the disaster minutes after the collapse. The staff braced for an onrush of victims. Blankets and mattresses were placed in the halls in preparation. Three doctors were on call at the time, and several others soon arrived. In all, seven victims were admitted to the hospital: five who were injured in the collapse and two who were in shock. The actions of the hospital staff during the emergency were exceptional. After his recovery, victim William Needham and his wife sent the hospital a thank you letter, which read in part: "Dear friends, we would like to thank you for everything wonderful you did for us while we were there. No words can express how we feel. It wasn't just the medical attention; it was the warm and friendly atmosphere of the entire hospital." (Photograph by Hobart Wilson; courtesy of Mike Miller.)

A great deal of debris ended up in the river. One of the more poignant sights of the disaster was of Christmas presents floating in the water. It was only a few weeks before the holiday, and some of the victims were on their way home from Christmas shopping. (Courtesy of Kay Sims Quimby.)

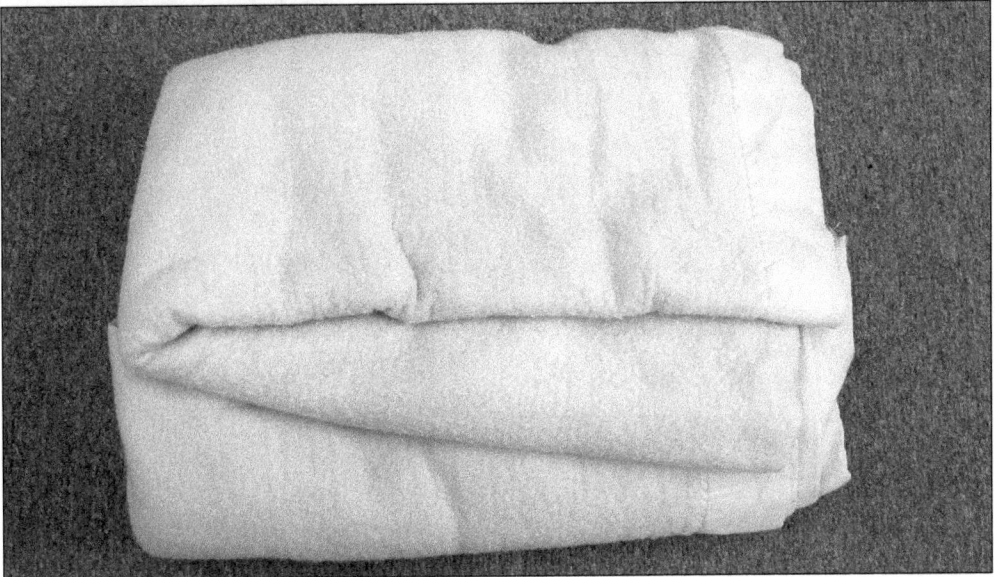

This blanket was recovered by Joe Tavan shortly after the collapse. Tavan worked at the Gallipolis Locks and Dams. He had just received word of the collapse and was bringing one of the derrick boats to the scene when he found the blanket in the river. (Courtesy of Paula Tavan Taylor.)

As word of the collapse spread, relatives and friends flocked to the site. Kay Sims Quimby (right, a few days later) remembers arriving at the scene and going numb. She, like many others, had assumed that only a portion of the bridge had fallen. When she regained her senses, she frantically, but fruitlessly, looked through the wreckage for her husband Ronald's white car. (Courtesy of Kay Sims Quimby.)

The night of the disaster was extremely cold, but rescue workers and anxious relatives worked around the clock. About 4:00 a.m., Dewey Keels was asked to take scrap wood and barrels to the site for fires. When the small amount of wood began to run out, Phil Foster, the owner of a nearby coal yard, donated a ton of coal to keep the fire burning. (Courtesy of PPRM.)

Three

AFTER THE FALL

In the aftermath of the collapse, a virtual army converged on the bridge site. During the first frantic hours, local agencies and volunteers gave as much aid as they could. As word of the tragedy reached higher authority levels, specialized units began to arrive and recovery efforts became more organized. Soon, the US Army Corps of Engineers took command. A control structure was developed so that each responding agency could make maximum use of their specialized capabilities. Numerous local volunteers also helped. Some locals contributed highly technical skills. Others simply gave the recovery teams a warm smile or a hot cup of coffee.

Recovery efforts were very efficient and successful. River navigation was reopened by December 21, and most large-scale recovery work was completed by the end of the month. All of the site work was finished by the beginning of February, although searches continued for missing bridge victims.

Point Pleasant, W.Va.

The dawn on December 16, 1967, brought cold, unflinching light to the disaster scene. Rescue workers and witnesses knew that the entire bridge had fallen, but not until the sun rose were they able to see the full extent of the tragedy. Only the piers, the approaches, and a small amount of twisted metal remained of the Silver Bridge. Most of the wreckage was submerged in the river and out of sight. Almost all of the visible onshore wreckage was in the debris pile on the Ohio shoreline. The aerial photograph above was taken over Point Pleasant, looking towards the Ohio side of the river. The below image shows the approach on the Ohio side and the debris pile. (Both, courtesy of Gallia Country Historical Genealogical Society.)

This was the sight that greeted recovery workers as they arrived at the Ohio side of the disaster site. The above photograph was taken from the railroad bridge looking toward the Silver Bridge approach. From this vantage point, almost the entire collapse area can be seen. A trail of tangled wreckage leads from the approach towards the river. Vehicles of rescue workers fill the bottomland near the bridge and the parking lot around Tiny's Foodland grocery store. The photograph below captures something of the feel of the disaster scene, as workers in the background struggle to move debris and dislodge vehicles. In the foreground, shocked spectators observe the scene and share the latest news. (Both, courtesy Cpl. Carl Boggs family.)

Traffic control was very important following the collapse. Routes 7 and 35 were heavily traveled, so drivers needed to be diverted around the blockage and directed to alternate routes. Here, an Ohio state trooper helps guide traffic through the area. Numerous signs warned drivers that the bridge was out. (Courtesy of Cpl. Carl Boggs family.)

The top of the Ohio bridge approach became literally the end of the road. The roadway remained intact up to the first bridge pier, but then separated abruptly at a joint between two sections of bridge decking. A straight line marked the transition between roadway and open space. (Courtesy of Cpl. Carl Boggs family.)

The bridge was relatively close to the ground on the Ohio side, so when the bridge collapsed, material in that area did not have far to fall. Most of the wreckage ended up in a compact, linear pile between the bridge pier and the shoreline. (Courtesy of Cpl. Carl Boggs family.)

This photograph examines some of the wreckage north of the Ohio-side bridge approach. The ribbon-like strips of metal are part of the eyebar suspension chain. The solid, linear bar in the foreground is one of the upright support columns that held the suspension chain in place. (Courtesy of the Gallia County Historical Genealogical Society.)

The devastation on the Ohio shoreline drew the eye of every newly arriving recovery worker and cameraman. The above image provides an overhead view of most of the debris pile. The photograph below illustrates the view at ground level. Damaged vehicles are scattered throughout the wreckage. Some fared better than others. The Haymans' red and black Pontiac sedan (below, center) is almost completely intact because it was partially shielded from the falling southern eyebar chain by the McLean Trucking Company truck. Other vehicles, like the Cantrells' station wagon, are heavily damaged. (Above, courtesy of Butch Brinker; below, courtesy of Cpl. Carl Boggs family.)

These are the remains of the North Carolina Transcon Line tractor-trailer. This was the last vehicle to land on the Ohio shoreline; those following it fell into the river. The truck came to rest so close to the waterline that most its trailer ended up in the water (above). Because it was so near the river, it is almost impossible to see in panoramic photographs of the debris field. The cab of the truck suffered massive damage (below). Operator Leo Blackman was killed and passenger John H. Fishel injured. (Above, courtesy of Cpl. Carl Boggs family; below, photograph by Hobart Wilson, courtesy of Mike Miller.)

The above photograph, taken from the southern side of the debris pile, provides an unusual view of three of the damaged vehicles. The McManus pickup truck is very prominent in the foreground. From this angle, the truck looks to be in good shape; however, the cab was almost completely crushed. To the left of the pickup is the bottom of the Cantrells' station wagon. At the far left is the McLean Trucking Company truck. The photograph below was taken from the Ohio-side bridge approach looking away from the disaster site towards Route 7. The rectangular white building is Tiny's Foodland grocery store. (Both, courtesy of PPRM.)

Relatively few ground-level photographs were taken of the collapse site on the West Virginia side of the river. Not only was there less physical debris there to attract the attention of cameramen, but the two sides of the bridge were also located in dramatically different environmental settings. The Ohio side was in open bottomland with few nearby buildings or obstructions, while the West Virginia side was in downtown Point Pleasant and ground-level views were largely blocked by buildings, trees, and the flood wall. This aerial view shows the features surrounding the West Virginia side of the bridge. Like on the Ohio side, the roadway on the West Virginia bridge approach remained intact up to the first pier, then abruptly ended at a joint between two sections of bridge decking. It was here that survivor Charlene Wood's car came to a stop right at the edge of the break. (Courtesy of USACE.)

These photographs provide views of the West Virginia bridge approach after the collapse. The above image looks toward the end of the approach from the base of the roadway. From this angle, the road appears to simply disappear into space. The image below was taken from the river during recovery operations when a great deal of activity was under way. At center, one of the M.T. Epling derrick boats recovers material from the river. In the foreground, a small vessel moves into position to drag for missing victims while spectators observe the proceedings from the riverbank. (Above, courtesy of Captain Charles H. Stone; below, courtesy of USACE.)

Above, West Virginia state trooper R.E. O'Dell stands on the edge of the West Virginia approach and stares into the void where the Silver Bridge used to be. Several ropes have been stretched across the roadway to serve as guardrails. In the background, derrick boats and small vessels conduct recovery operations. Trooper O'Dell played several important roles during the disaster. In addition to assisting with rescue operations, he personally placed location and time of recovery tags on 26 of the deceased bridge victims. O'Dell is seen at right several years after the disaster. (Above, courtesy of Cpl. Carl Boggs family; right, courtesy of Rudy E. Odell.)

61

Few visible remains were left of the central portion of the bridge. Behind the derrick boat (above), an intact section of roadway runs from the top of the central bridge pier into the river. From this angle, the roadway section appears almost vertical. However, in other photographs, like the one below, it is clear that it enters the water at about a 50-degree angle. At the time of the collapse, the Ford sedan of Denzil and Glenna Mae Taylor was in the lane nearest the camera, approximately at the level of the waterline. (Above, courtesy of Cpl. Carl Boggs family; below, courtesy of Darlene Haer.)

Emergency workers divide disaster management into several phases. Two of the most important are the rescue and recovery phases. Rescue efforts take place while victims are alive and remain in danger. Actions taken during the rescue phase are aimed at finding and saving these people. Recovery operations begin when there is no longer any hope of finding living victims. During the Silver Bridge collapse, river-based rescue operations lasted only a few minutes because of the low water temperatures and the fact that many vehicles ended up heavily damaged and submerged. Shore-based rescue operations lasted somewhat longer. (Above, courtesy of Cpl. Carl Boggs family; below, courtesy of Darlene Haer.)

Ohio Tower

Ohio Chan Bent

15 Panels at 25'-4" = 380'-0"   28 Panels at 25'-0" = 700'-0"

ELEVATION

Ohio State Route 7

TRAFFIC PLAN

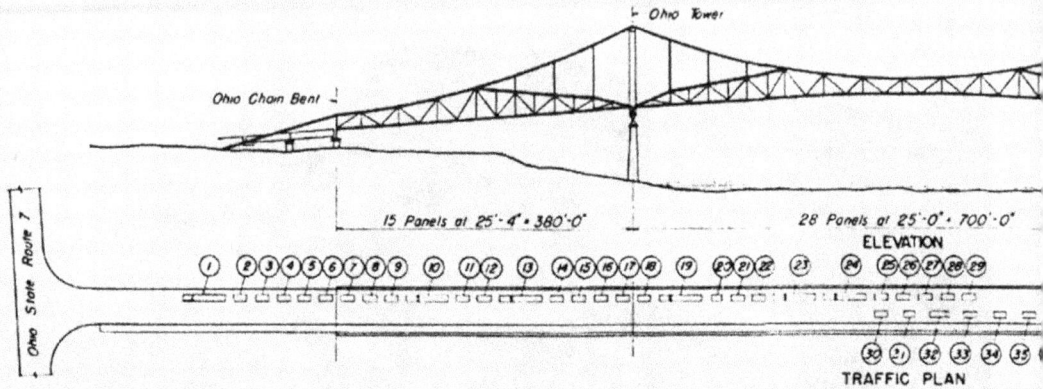

VEHICLE NO	GROSS WT	LICENSE NO	VEHICLE TYPE				OWNER	VEHICLE	
			YEAR	MAKE	COLOR	MODEL		OPERATOR	
1		W Va 857037 / W Va C/9	1967 / 1958	International Trailmobile	White	COE Single axle Tractor Tdm axle Semitrailer	Davis Wholesale Trucking Co	Meadows, Garry E	Murp
2		Ohio Z1991H	1959	Chevrolet	Tan	2 Dr Sedan	Sanders, Donovan	Sanders, Donovan	None
3		W Va 90860	1962	Dodge Dart	Buff/Brown	4 Dr Sedan	Rader, Howard J	Rader, Howard J.	None
4		Ohio Z92J	1967	Buick	Blue	4 Dr Sedan	Bingham, Alfred C	Bingham, Alfred C	Ram.
5		Ohio Z434J	1966	Chrysler	White	Sedan	Spann, W B Jr	Spann, W B Jr	None
6		Ohio 1825J	1964	Ford	Black	Sedan	Belville, Ralph	Belville, Ralph	None
7	5,660	Ohio 2774N	1967	Chevrolet	Flame/Brown	Sedan Caprice	Fowler, James	Fowler, John W	Fowler/Nichol
8	3,900	Ky 579-542	1960	Chevrolet	White/Brown	2 Dr Sedan	McCleese, Dewey O	McCleese, Dewey O	None
9	6,200	Ohio Z6185	1955	Pontiac	Black/Red	2 Dr Sedan	Hayman, Paul	Hayman, Paul M.	Haym.
10	48,103	NC 2665 / NC 896KB	1965 / 1967	White Trailmobile	Red	COE Tdm axle Tractor Tdm axle Semitrailer	McLean Trucking Co	Nunn, Francis O. (I)	Ellis
11	3,366	W Va 915-939	1959	Rambler	(U)	Station Wagon	Cantrell, Margaret Mrs	Cantrell, Margaret Mrs (I)	Cantr
12	6,200	Ohio 406572	1965	Ford	(U)	3/4 Ton Pickup Truck	Eliose McManus	McManus, Gerald (F)	None
13	69,701	N Carolina	1962 / 1963	White Strich	(U)	COE Tdm axle Tractor Tdm axle Semitrailer	Transcon Lines	Blackman, Leo (F)	Fishe
14	4,300	Ohio Z385J	1961	Pontiac	(U)	Sedan	Cremeans, Horace	Cremeans, Donald Horace (F)	Lane,
15	4,000	Ohio 283LL	1956	Chevrolet	(U)	Convertable	Lewis, Bruce	Wamsley, Marvin Landy (F)	Case,
16	4,600	Ohio 2753K	1965	Buick	Blue	Sedan	Carpenter, Margaret	Smith, Charles T. (F)	Smith
17	4,200	W Va 133-921	1968	Chevrolet	(U)	Sedan	White, James Alfred	White, James Alfred (F)	Nona
18	4,600	Ohio Z1842J	1967	Pontiac	(U)	Sedan, Tudor Hardtop	Sims, Ronald R.	Head, Robert (F)	Sims,
19	64,720	NC 6321 / NC 523FA	1966 / 1964	White Trailmobile	(U)	COE Tdm axle Tractor Tdm axle Semitrailer	Hennis Freight Lines, Inc	Edmondson, William M (I)	Cund
20	1,900	Ohio Z70L	1965	Volks Wagon	(U)	Sedan	Adler, E. Albert Jr.	Adler, Albert E Jr. (F)	None
21	2,600	Ohio Z252C	1962	Ford Falcon	(U)	Station Wagon	Ohio Valley Publishing Co	Cantrell, Thomas Allen (F)	None
22	4,000	Ohio Z1046J	1965	Chevrolet	(U)	2 Dr Sedan	Boggs, Howard J	Boggs, Howard J. (I)	Boggs
23	51,327	Del C48394	1966 / 1961	Mack Ginds	(U)	COE Tdm axle Tractor Tdm axle Semitrailer	Roadway Express Co	Mabe, Gene Harold (F)	Benne
24	59,308	NC 44569	1965 / 1961	GMC Ginds	(U)	COE Tdm axle Tractor Tdm axle Semitrailer	Roadway Express Co	Needham, William N. Jr (I)	Towe,
25	4,400	Ohio Z677D	1965	Dodge	(U)	2 Dr Sedan	Pullen, James O. and Pullen, Roberta E.	Pullen, James O. (F)	Milla
26	4,000	Ohio D5209	1965	Ford	(U)	Sedan	Firestone Tire and Rubber Co	Hawkins, James W (F)	None
27	4,200	W V J-224	1961	Ford (Taxi)	(U)	Sedan	Pickens Cab Company	Sanders, Leo Otto (F)	Moore
28	3,200	Ohio Z935M	1962	Rambler	(U)	Sedan	Wray, Christine	Maxwell, James Richard (F)	None
29	3,900	Ohio Z703J	1962	Chevrolet	Green	Sedan	Deem, Gertrude	Lee, Thomas Howard (F)	None
30	4,500	W Va 499-571	1962	Ford	(U)	Station Wagon	Turner, Victor William	Turner, Victor William (F)	Turne
31	3,400	W Va 520-065	1965	Ford Mustang	(U)	Sedan, Tudor Hardtop	Byrus, Hilda G.	Byrus, Hilda G (F)	Byrus
32	48,100	Ohio 13J25	1965	International	Red	Tdm axle Dump Truck	Robert R Greene Hauling	Higley, Forest R (F)	None
33	4,300	W Va 290-662	1959	Pontiac	(U)	Sedan, Fordor	Nibert, Nora I	Nibert, Nora Isabelle (F)	North
34	4,600	W Va 92-864	1961	Oldsmobile	(U)	Sedan	Wedge, Paul D.	Wedge, Paul D (F)	Wedge
35	4,600	W Va 499-941	1955	Chevrolet	(U)	Sedan	Meadows, James F.	Meadows, James Franklin (F)	Duff,
36	4,200	W Va 359-820	1965	Ford	Red	Sedan	Taylor, Denzil Ray	Taylor, Denzil (F)	Taylor
37	48,300	Ohio 13C-911	1967	Chevrolet	Red	Tdm axle Dump Truck	Robert R Greene Hauling	Doral, Alonzo (F)	Wams
38		Ohio Z1737K	1964	Pontiac	Black over White	Sedan 2 Door	Wood, Carlos	Wood, Charlene	Nona

64

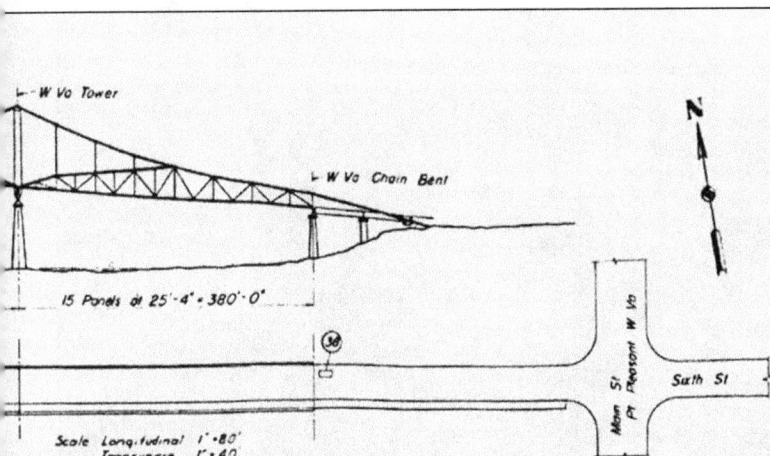

Labels on the drawing:

W Va Tower

W Va Chain Bent

15 Panels at 25'-4" = 380'-0"

Scale Longitudinal 1" = 80'
Transverse 1" = 40'

N

Main St
Pt Pleasant W Va

Sixth St

PASSENGER(S)

Chapman, Judith

...dg; Craig, Harold
Mrs

1; Counts, Cecil (F)

(F)

); Sturgeon, Maxine Ellen (F)

(F); Boggs, Kristye
er (F)

(F)

(F); Scott, Paul A (I)

Mayes, Darlene (F)
(F); Byrus, Kathy (F)

(F)

r (F)

F); Meadows, Timothy F. (F)

Legend
(I) Injury
(F) Fatality
(U) Unknown
COE - Cab Over Engine

U. S. DEPARTMENT OF TRANSPORTATION
NATIONAL TRANSPORTATION SAFETY BOARD
WASHINGTON D C

OHIO RIVER BRIDGE
AT POINT PLEASANT, WEST VIRGINIA

TRAFFIC DATA SHEET

DATE
May 1968

This US Department of Transportation technical drawing serves as a priceless Rosetta Stone for the Silver Bridge disaster. Using it as a basic site guide, it is possible to instantly determine where individual photographs were taken and where witnesses and victims were positioned during the collapse. Lateral- and vertical-scale representations of the bridge are provided, and the location of every vehicle is precisely indicated. The highly detailed legend lists the make and model of each vehicle, along with its license plate number, owner, operator, and passengers. It also records the fate of each vehicle occupant. (Courtesy of the National Transportation Safety Board.)

65

Most survivors were found in the debris pile on the Ohio shore (above). Of the 17 victims who ended up on the shoreline, four died. In contrast, only five of the 47 people who fell into the river survived. The photograph below, taken a few days after the collapse, illustrates how rescue workers made use of the bottomland on the Ohio side of the river. The flat space between the Silver Bridge approach and the railroad bridge made an ideal staging site for rescue and recovery operations. Vehicles from many different organizations are visible. (Above, courtesy of Cpl. Carl Boggs family; below, courtesy of Gallia Country Historical Genealogical Society.)

Recovery operations began as soon as the last survivors were removed from the scene. Several major tasks presented themselves. First, vehicles and victims needed to be recovered. Second, given that the Ohio River played a vital role in regional commerce, it was critical to remove obstacles and reopen the river to commercial traffic. Third, all bridge material had to be recovered so that a full investigation into the collapse could be conducted. Finally, search operations had to be performed to locate any missing victims, vehicles, or key pieces of debris. (Above, courtesy of Gallia County Historical Genealogical Society; below, courtesy of Butch Brinker.)

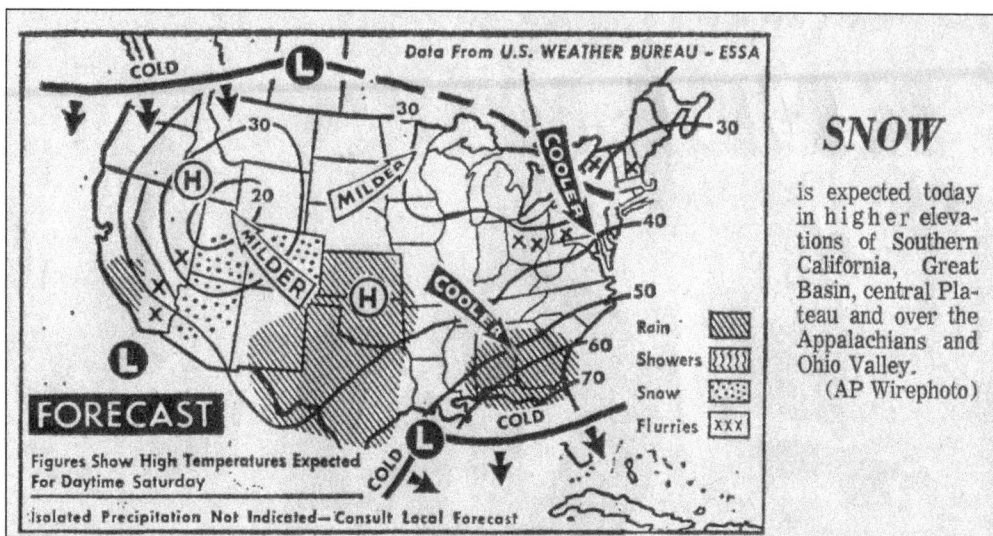

This chart shows the national weather forecast for December 16, 1967. Temperatures dropped sharply after the disaster, but weather conditions remained very good for the first six days of operations. After that, it became extremely cold with frequent freezing rain, sleet, and snow. At times, precipitation reduced visibility to less than a mile. The terrible weather greatly frustrated recovery operations. (Courtesy of the *Charleston Gazette*.)

Snow covers the Ohio shoreline several weeks after the disaster. A path has been worn to the river by recovery workers and spectators. Only a small amount of wreckage is visible; by this time, most of the large debris had been removed. (Courtesy of Terry Raike Burnett.)

After the collapse, numerous federal and local agencies converged on the area to help coordinate recovery operations. These agencies included the US Army Corps of Engineers, the US Coast Guard, the Mason County and Gallia County Civil Defense Units, West Virginia and Ohio state police, the National Guard, the US Department of Transportation, the US Department of Natural Resources, the US Bureau of Public Roads, and various agencies of the State of West Virginia. Many local citizens also volunteered their services. The US Army Corps of Engineers was nominally in charge of all operations related to the bridge scene itself. The Coast Guard handled river traffic. Other agencies acted in a supportive role, though many were given oversight of specific tasks. Much of the actual recovery work was undertaken by contractors with expertise in underwater recovery and salvage. (Courtesy of USACE.)

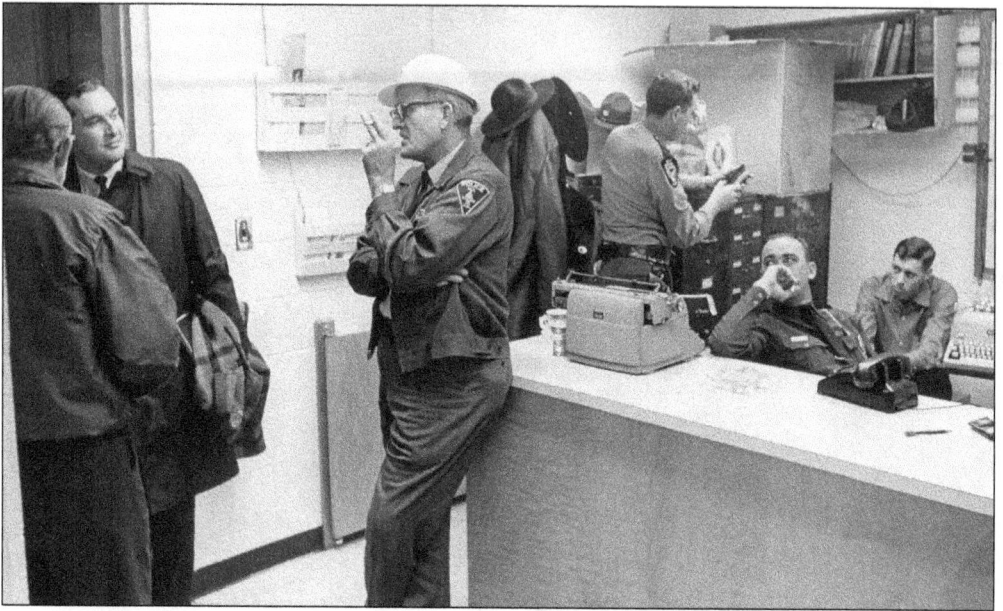

John "Andy" Wilson (center, in white hard hat) was the director of the Mason County Civil Defense Unit and coordinated recovery efforts on the West Virginia side of the river. Wilson's counterpart on the Ohio side was John Epling. The fact that the two ends of the Silver Bridge were in separate states added a unique logistical challenge to the recovery efforts. (Courtesy of Carolyn Wilson.)

Recovery work was aided by excellent communications. A high-quality, interdepartmental communication system was in place before the disaster. This system allowed complex decisions to be made quickly and let critical information get to workers in the field. This photograph shows officials coordinating operations at the command center. Andy Wilson is in the white hard hat, and John Epling is standing. Note the numerous phone lines. (Courtesy of Carolyn Wilson.)

Systematic recovery operations began in the early afternoon of December 16, 1967. By this time, derrick boats and their support vessels from the M.T. Epling Company and the Dravo Corporation had arrived at the scene. They quickly got to work recovering the sunken vehicles from the collapse. (Courtesy of USACE.)

The disaster scene posed daunting challenges to recovery workers and accident investigators as bridge wreckage was in the river and on both shorelines. All debris needed to be located, recovered, and cataloged. In addition, the site had to be secured and road and river traffic reopened. Here, police officers on the Ohio side take a much-needed break from their duties. (Courtesy of Terry Raike Burnett.)

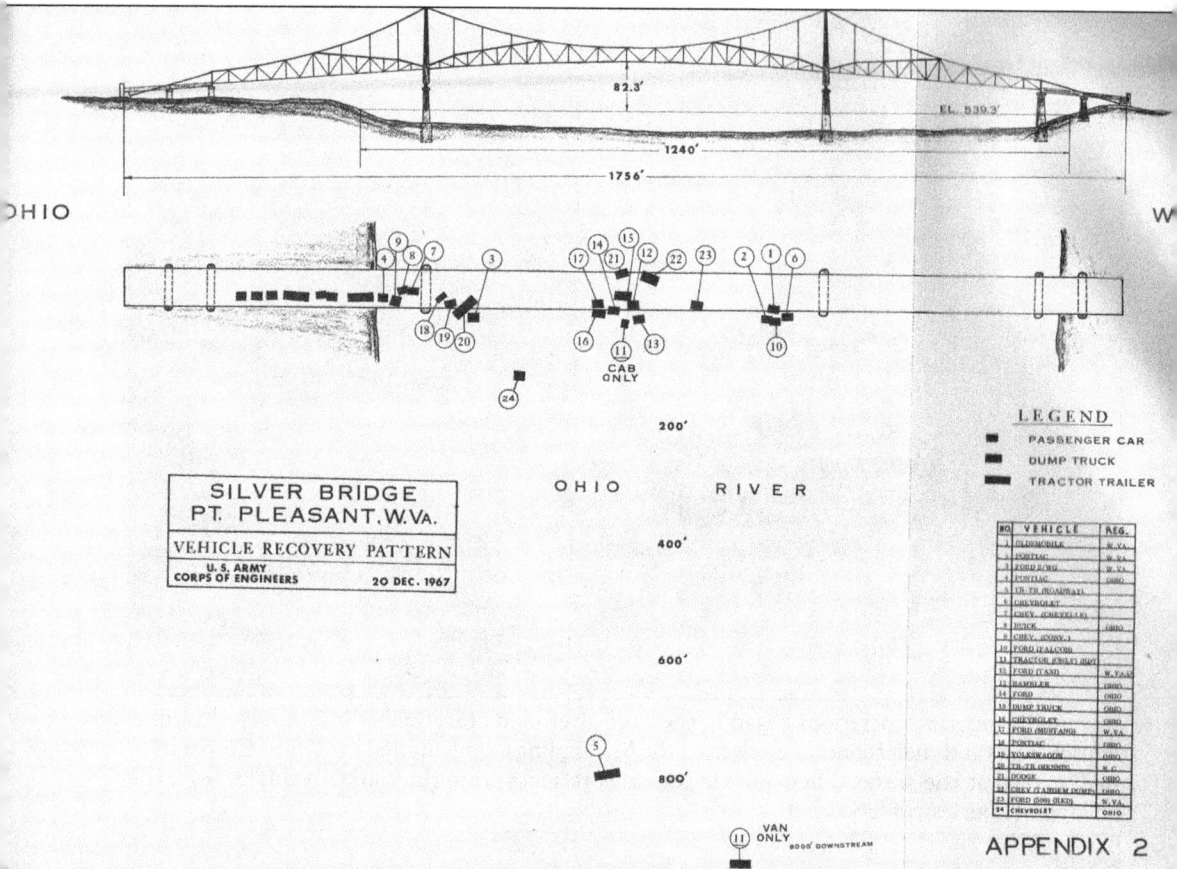

SILVER BRIDGE
PT. PLEASANT, W.VA.

VEHICLE RECOVERY PATTERN

U.S. ARMY
CORPS OF ENGINEERS   20 DEC. 1967

82.3'   EL. 539.3'
1240'
1756'
OHIO   W

OHIO   RIVER

200'
400'
600'
800'

CAB ONLY
VAN ONLY   8000' DOWNSTREAM

LEGEND
■ PASSENGER CAR
■ DUMP TRUCK
■ TRACTOR TRAILER

NO	VEHICLE	REG.
1	OLDSMOBILE	W.VA.
2	PONTIAC	W.VA.
3	FORD (CW)	W.VA.
4	PONTIAC	OHIO
5	TR-TR (ROADWAY)	
6	CHEVROLET	
7	CHEV. (CHEVELLE)	
8	BUICK	OHIO
9	CHEV. (ENVY.)	
10	FORD (FALCON)	
11	TRACTOR (ONLY) (DUMP)	
12	FORD (T.AND)	W.VA.
13	RAMBLER	OHIO
14	FORD	OHIO
15	DUMP TRUCK	OHIO
16	CHEVROLET	OHIO
17	FORD (MUSTANG)	W.VA.
18	PONTIAC	OHIO
19	VOLKSWAGON	OHIO
20	TR-TR (HIGHWAY)	N.C.
21	DODGE	OHIO
22	CHEV. (TANDEM DUMP)	OHIO
23	FORD (500) (OLDS)	W.VA.
24	CHEVROLET	OHIO

APPENDIX 2

Of the 31 vehicles that fell with the bridge, 24 ended up in the river. Locating and recovering sunken vehicles was the top priority of recovery teams. Many vehicles were entangled in the wreckage and came to rest within the original footprint of the bridge. A few, however, ended up a considerable distance downstream. Vehicles were located by divers and by specially equipped boats mounting fathometers and sonar equipment. Metal detectors were also used, but it is unclear if these were boat mounted, diver operated, or both. By December 31, all but one vehicle had been found. The last car, the 1965 Chevrolet of the Boggs family, was recovered on January 27, 1968. This detailed map constructed by the US Army Corps of Engineers illustrates the recovery location of every sunken vehicle. Only the vehicles that were submerged are numbered. Those in the Ohio-side debris pile are not. (Courtesy of USACE.)

Once vehicles were located, derrick boats lifted them from the river and loaded them onto barges. One of the most effective recovery methods was for divers to locate the submerged wrecks and then have derrick boats lift them with clamshell buckets (above). An alternative method was for divers to attach slings to the vehicles (below). As with many recovery photographs, it is not possible to tell which vehicles are being recovered in these pictures. Both of these cars show the type of extensive damage inflicted by the bridge collapse. Most vehicles did not simply fall into the river; they were also hit by falling debris. (Both, courtesy of USACE.)

Above, a damaged car is carefully lifted from the river. In many cases, victim's bodies were not removed from the vehicles until they were out of the water, so special care had to be taken during recovery to make sure the vehicles were handled as gently as possible. (Courtesy of Gallia Country Historical Genealogical Society.)

The remains of the Picken's Cab Company taxi are loaded onto a recovery barge. Both occupants, driver Lee "Doc" Otto Sanders and rider Ronald Gene Moore, were killed. When Moore's body was recovered, he still held the $1 bill he had intended to use for his fare. (Courtesy of Jim Roach family.)

The recovery barges were locally available coal barges, which were quite large and could hold many vehicles. The barge above has at least four cars loaded and still has considerable space left for more. Once removed from the river and inspected for victims, the vehicles were transported to a collection point on the West Virginia side of the river (below), about 1.5 miles north of the bridge site. In 1967, the area was owned by the General Services Administration. The site now houses the Defense National Stockpile Center Point Pleasant depot. (Above, courtesy of USACE; below, courtesy of PPRM.)

Volunteers search the wreckage for bodies. Several locals, including William "Slim" Wilcox and Earl Starkey (not pictured), helped remove bodies from the vehicles. Wilcox and Starkey were working at the Marietta Manufacturing Plant when officials arrived and asked for volunteers who would be willing to go through the vehicles and remove victim remains. Out of a sense of duty to the dead, both agreed. (Courtesy of Gallia County Historical Genealogical Society.)

Photographs of the bodies were not permitted. Official governmental photographers did not take pictures of the victims, and police asked civilians not to photograph vehicles with bodies inside. When an overzealous cameraman ignored this request, a frustrated deputy threw the man's camera into the river. (Courtesy of Gallia County Historical Genealogical Society.)

Dr. C. Leonard Brown and nurse Melba Brown helped set up a morgue at the National Guard Armory (below). They then worked together to process and care for the dead. Dr. Brown was a local physician who had served in Korea. His services were very much in demand because of his previous experience with multi-casualty situations. The Browns' daughter Nancy remembers, "They were always quiet and you could see the veil of sadness over them as they returned home each day. They were happy to be able to serve their community, but were sad for the circumstances." (Right, courtesy of Alice Click; below, courtesy of Tom O'Dell.)

Professional divers played a major role in the recovery operations. Divers came from the US Army Corps of Engineers and from Marine Contracting International, Inc., based in Southport, Connecticut. The divers were tasked with several important missions, including acting as the eyes for surface units and surveying and mapping the entire underwater collapse site. They also assisted the derrick boats by pinpointing the position of submerged vehicles and wreckage and attaching slings for their removal. Here, surface support workers assist a diver after a dive, helping him remove his gear while he describes the conditions below. (Both, courtesy of Gallia County Historical Genealogical Society.)

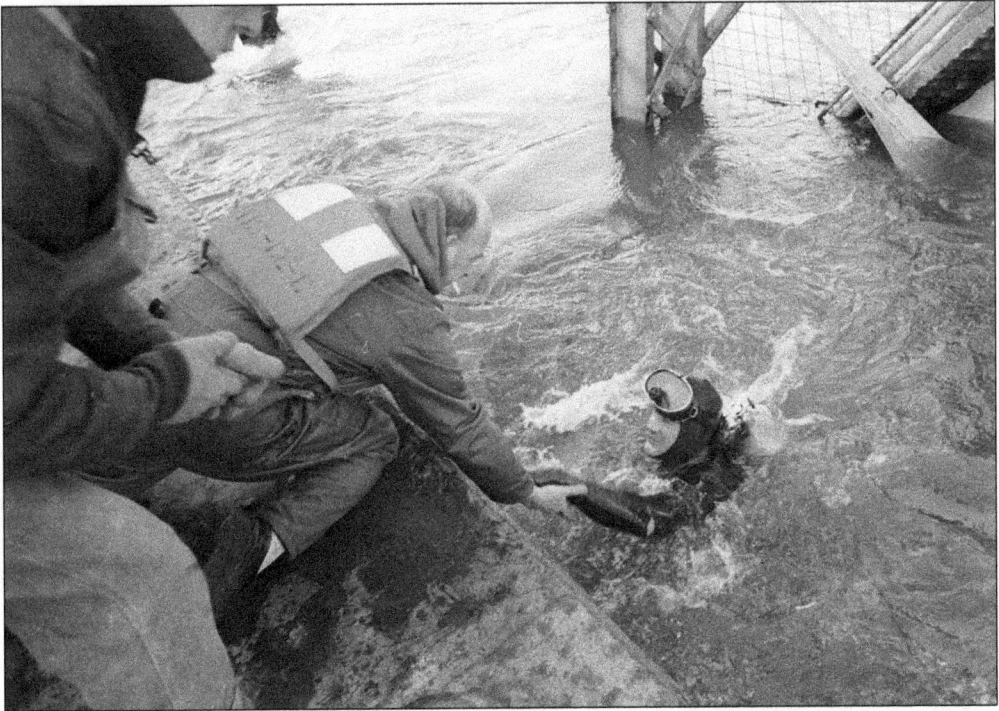

Diving operations were exceptionally hazardous. Almost every possible underwater challenge was present. The current was strong. The water was cold, usually between 40 and 44 degrees. Visibility was very poor; often divers could only see a few inches. And lastly, the work was conducted in a hazardous maze of twisted, moving metal. (Courtesy of *Herald Dispatch*.)

Diver Max Ray underscored the hazardous conditions in an interview with a local newspaper, saying, "It's real hairy and dangerous down there. You've got to worry about metal falling on you. You can't see your hand on the face plate of your mask. It's so dark, pitch black." (Courtesy of Jim Roach family.)

Extensive dragging operations were conducted to locate the bodies of missing bridge victims. Though critical, dragging was a grueling, time-consuming task. To drag, small boats motored slowly back and forth across the river pulling long lines fitted with grapples. It was hoped that the grapples would snag victims or pieces of bridge debris. Often nothing was found, while at other times, grapples would snag submerged material unrelated to the disaster. A single boat could cover only a very small area (above), so many boats were deployed simultaneously (below) to increase the odds of finding victims. (Both, courtesy of USACE.)

Dragging was coordinated by the Coast Guard and Civil Defense authorities, but the actual work was carried out by volunteers. Dragging started very soon after the collapse and continued—weather permitting—for several months. Volunteers came from many sources, including but not limited to, the Gallipolis Boat Club; civil defense workers from Auglaize County, Butler County, Carrol County, Clark County, Gallipolis, and Shelby County; firemen from Charleston, the Dayton 21 Fire Department, Dunbar, Gallipolis, Kingston, Mechanicsburg, Middleport, Nitro, Point Peasant, Pomeroy, Racine, Ravenswood, Ripley, South Charleston, Spencer Cottageville, St. Albans, Syracuse, and West Milton; and independent volunteers from many neighboring communities. (Courtesy of USACE.)

Crowds of spectators were common on both sides of the river during the recovery period. Most of the people were locals, though newsmen and incident investigators were also present. People were drawn to the site out of a sense of curiosity. Many had friends or relatives involved in the disaster, and some knew people who were still missing. The mood of the crowds varied, but it was usually a mixture of reverence, curiosity, and sadness. Onlookers line the riverbank at Point Pleasant (above) and Route 7 on the Ohio side of the river (below). (Above, courtesy of USACE; below, courtesy of Butch Brinker.)

A great deal of the work—and virtually all of the heavy lifting—was accomplished by derrick boats and their support vessels. Derrick boats were essentially floating cranes, able to easily move around the disaster site and remove material with pinpoint accuracy. Initially, they focused their efforts on recovering sunken vehicles but soon undertook the job of collecting bridge wreckage. A Dravo Corporation derrick boat (above) works the mid-river near a central bridge pier, while an M.T. Epling derrick boat (below) works close to the West Virginia shore. The derrick boats were very conspicuous at the collapse site; many photographs show their distinctive cranes poking up in the background. (Both, courtesy of Darlene Haer.)

One of the more interesting vehicles used in the recovery operation were Civil Defense unit DUKWs, commonly called "ducks." DUKWs were amphibious trucks developed during World War II for use during amphibious assaults and for logistical support. After the war, some DUKWs ended up in local jurisdictions and were used by emergency services. (Courtesy of Robert Keathley.)

Here, an amphibious DUWK hauls itself out on the riverbank. Rhonda Sims Dixon remembers that the DUWK drivers, as well as the professional divers, would visit their home and update the family on the recovery progress and the search for their missing father, Ronald Sims. In return, the family would provide snacks to the cold, tired men. (Courtesy of Kay Sims Quimby.)

To determine the cause of the collapse, investigators attempted to collect all of the wreckage from the Silver Bridge. Once recovered, bridge pieces were transported to this bottomland, about 1.5 miles downstream from the bridge site adjacent to Henderson, West Virginia (seen here in 2012). Here, in a manner similar to the way aircraft are reconstructed after a crash, bridge wreckage was laid out and partially reassembled. Debris recovery efforts were very successful. For example, approximately 90 percent of the bridge deck was collected. This area has changed significantly in the 44 years since the disaster. Although this portion of the field looks more or less as it did in 1967, the photograph was taken from the raised approach to the Silver Memorial Bridge—the bridge built to replace the Silver Bridge. (Courtesy of Stephan Bullard.)

Above, a group of bridge eyebars, some with connecting pins still attached, are lined up at the Henderson, West Virginia, recovery site. The shafts of all of these eyebars show some deformation from the collapse, but the heads remain intact. The image below illustrates the type of wreckage typically recovered with fragments of concrete bridge decking and pieces of steel visible. It is unclear exactly where this photograph was taken, but given that the trees are damaged, it must be at the collapse site. (Above, courtesy of Butch Brinker; below, courtesy of Kay Sims Quimby.)

After the tragedy, victims and their families did their best to return to their normal lives. Here, Paul A. Scott walks his daughter Carol Scott Bachtel down the aisle on December 30, 1967, only 15 days after the fall of the bridge. Scott was riding in James Pullen's Dodge when the bridge collapsed. His right arm is still bandaged from the disaster. (Courtesy of Carol Scott Bachtel.)

Friends helped as best they could. Kristy Blazer Woodall, 15 years old at the time, remembers going with her family to take food to the widow and small sons of Dean Miller. When they rang the doorbell, the two Miller boys came running, yelling, "Daddy! Daddy! Is it Daddy?" Mrs. Miller said that the boys ran to the door like that every time someone visited. (Courtesy of Linda Lane.)

Five-year-old twins Ronda and Tammy Sims open presents on Christmas morning in 1967. Their father, Ronald Sims, was still missing from the bridge collapse. Despite her best intentions, the twins' distraught mother, Kay, had been unable to prepare for the holiday. In a greatly appreciated act of kindness, the Goodyear Tire and Rubber Company and local churches pitched in to provide the family with presents. The devastating tragedy, which happened so close to the holiday, compelled many people to help affected families. For example, the City of Huntington contributed toys, food, clothing, 1,000 pounds of fruit, and $800 in cash. These items were delivered to the Presbyterian church in Point Pleasant and Grace Methodist Church in Gallipolis. Church officials and civic groups helped distribute the gifts. Ronda Sims and her mother remember that the girls received dolls and bicycles that Christmas. To this day, they remain touched by the compassion the community showed them during this terrible time. (Courtesy of Kay Sims Quimby.)

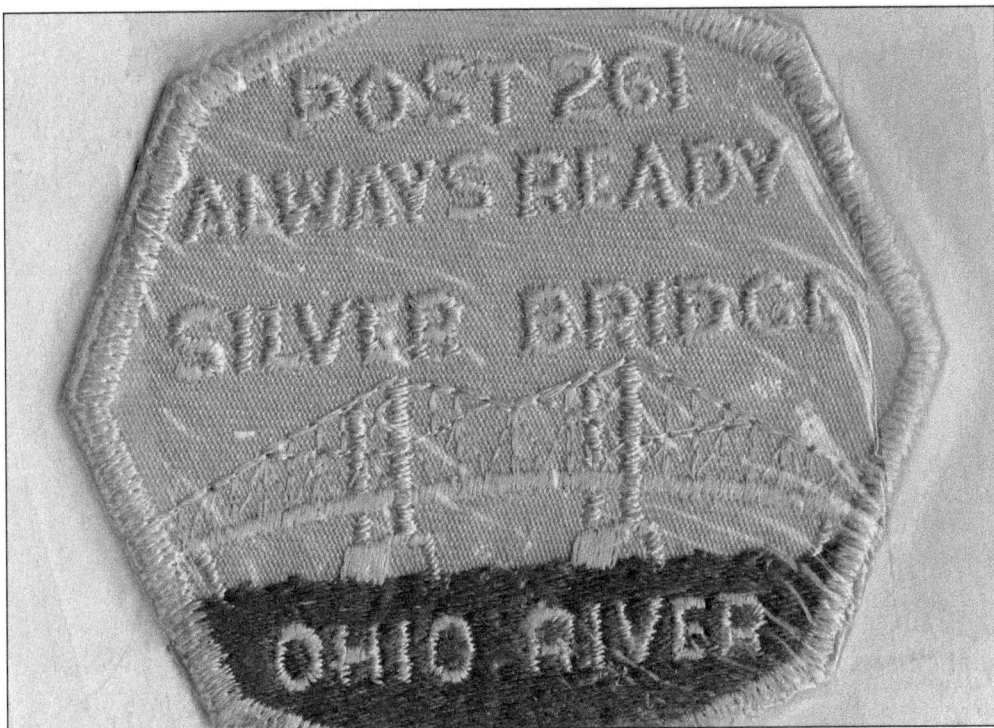

Almost everyone helped in some way. Under the leadership of Ken Leikari, local Boy Scouts of America Post 261 spent 10 days assisting relief agencies. In honor of their efforts, Post 261 was awarded the prestigious Ready Reserve Award. Bruce and Greg Adkins (ages 14 and 16 at the time) designed this patch to commemorate their work. Only 220 copies were produced. (Courtesy of Greg and Bruce Adkins.)

Major operations began to wind down towards the end of December. The US Army Corps of Engineers Emergency Operations Center closed on December 29, and the field office and communications center at Point Pleasant were closed on December 31. Work continued—especially the search for missing bridge victims—but on a somewhat smaller scale. (Courtesy of George McClintock.)

Overall, recovery and removal operations were time consuming and costly. A total of 15,379 man-hours were spent on recovery operations, not including volunteer labor. Operations were conducted around the clock with most personnel working 12-hour shifts. During the time of peak operations—the greatest activity was on December 20—a total of 97 people were directly working at the scene. By the end of the month, this number dropped to an average of around 50 people per day. In terms of cost, from December 15, 1967, to February 5, 1968, a total of $235,315.11 was spent on disaster-related expenses. This included, among other budget items, $46,449 in direct labor costs; $23,478 for the use of watercraft, including the derrick boats; and $140,234 in contractor fees. Though seemingly small by modern standards, these were exceptionally high expenses in 1968. (Photograph by Hobart Wilson; courtesy of Mike Miller.)

Four

THE CAUSE OF THE COLLAPSE

After the collapse, there was a great deal of speculation about why the Silver Bridge fell. Some suggested that inferior steel had been used to make the bridge. Others thought that too many heavy trucks had been on the bridge at one time. A few suggested that the bridge was destroyed as an act of sabotage. To determine the cause of the collapse, the National Bureau of Standards undertook one of the most thorough incident investigations ever mounted. In the end, all hypotheses were disproved except for one.

The cause of the collapse was related to the bridge's innovative design. The direct cause was the failure of eyebar number 330 on the northern side of the bridge near the Ohio side of the river. Undetected stress corrosion cracks had developed on the head of this eyebar. These cracks had been present and growing for at least a few years. Eventually, one became deep enough—about 1/8 of an inch—to completely fracture the steel eyebar. Because the eyebars on each side of the bridge were linked together in a chain, the failure of one led to the catastrophic collapse of the entire side and then the whole bridge. Even though the cracks had been present for some time, there was no way to detect them during inspections because of where they were located.

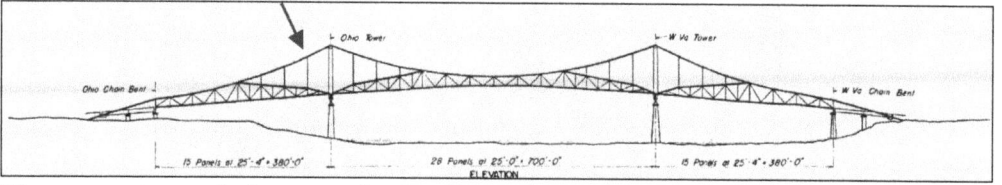

The arrow points to the location of eyebar 330 on the northern (upstream) side of the bridge. Its exact location was at joint 13, north bar, north chain, Ohio-side span, at the first parallel point, about 50 feet west of the Ohio tower. (Courtesy of USACE, arrow added.)

The eyebars that formed the suspension chains were long steel beams with circular heads, or "eyes," at both ends. They were 12 inches wide, two inches thick, and varied in length depending on where they were in the chain. Few Silver Bridge eyebars survive today, but this one and its connecting pin are housed in the Point Pleasant River Museum. (Courtesy of Stephan Bullard.)

This photograph, taken from the center of the bridge looking towards the West Virginia side, shows the relative thinness of the suspension eyebars. At first glance, the bridge appears to be supported by traditional wire cables, however, that was just the way the eyebar chains looked from below. (Courtesy of PPRM.)

Each segment of suspension chain was composed of two parallel eyebars. At every connection point, four eyebars converged and were linked together by a single pin. This photograph shows the arrangement, where a fallen portion of the chain provides an almost top-down view of a connection point. (Courtesy of Cpl. Carl Boggs family.)

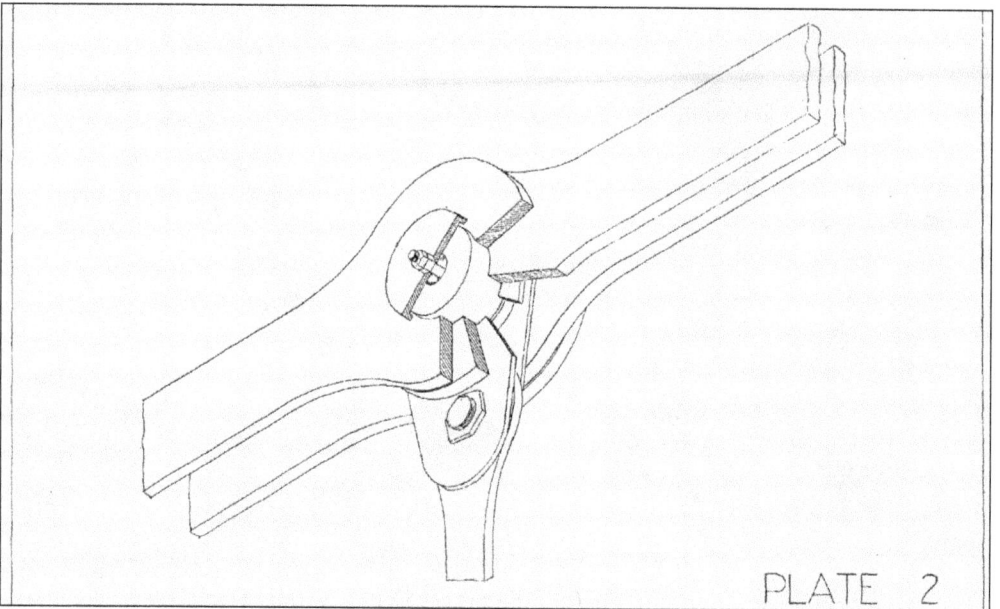

Here, a typical eyebar chain connection joint is illustrated. This drawing shows how the connections were formed and illustrates the spatial relationships between structural members. Several different types of connection joints were used on the Silver Bridge for different portions of the chain. (Courtesy of the National Transportation Safety Board.)

Because eyebar's heads overlapped at connection points, large portions of many eyebars were concealed from view, making it impossible for inspectors to see the hidden parts of the eyebars when the chains were suspended above the bridge. This allowed undetected corrosion to develop on the eyebars. (Courtesy of Jim Roach family.)

Investigators examine part of an eyebar chain at the Henderson, West Virginia, recovery site. After the collapse, each bridge piece was meticulously examined to determine its point of origin and to see if it had been damaged. The pieces shown here represent an anchor point for one of the suspension chains. The eyebars fit into the large slotted section at left. The connecting pin does not appear to be present. This photograph gives a good impression of the size of the eyebars. At ground level, with people serving as a reference point, the eyebars seem quite large. However, compared with the other bridge elements, they are relatively small and thin. The photograph also illustrates the parallel structure of the eyebars that formed each chain and the large "eyes" at the end of each eyebar. The upper eyebar has been slightly deformed by the collapse. (Courtesy of the *Herald-Dispatch*.)

This photograph shows workers constructing the southern eyebar chain during the building of the Silver Bridge. Eyebar 330 has not yet been installed, but it will be placed high up on the north chain, almost directly behind where the seated man is working. The initial installation of the eyebar chains was especially dangerous. (Courtesy of USACE.)

A section of the eyebar chain lies across the ruins of the Ohio-side bridge approach. Many of the eyebars in the southern chain remained connected after the collapse; several reports claim that the chain ran uninterrupted all the way to West Virginia. (Courtesy of Cpl. Carl Boggs family.)

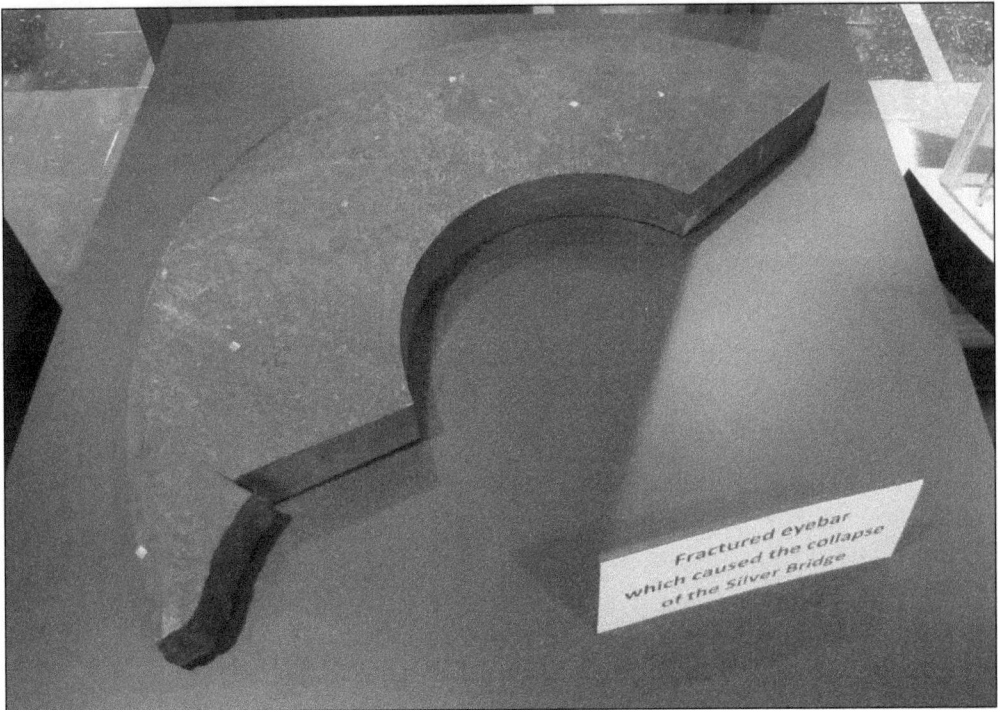

These are the remains of eyebar 330, the failure of which caused the collapse of the Silver Bridge. The initial break occurred on the "straight" side of the eyebar (above, right). The fracture site is almost linear because once the crack reached its critical depth, that side of the head broke almost instantaneously. The fracture line is artificially smooth (below) because a small portion has been removed for structural analysis. The opposite side of the eyebar exhibits jagged deformation. When the opposite side of the eyebar cracked, an unsupportable load transferred to the metal on this side. It did not have the strength to hold up the bridge, and the metal was deformed as it tore loose from the connecting pin. Today, the eyebar is housed in the Museum of the National Institute of Standards and Technology in Gaithersburg, Maryland. (Both, courtesy of Stephan Bullard.)

POSSIBLE CAUSES OF FAILURE

Substructure
- Anchorage Move
- Pier Displacement
- Pier Scour

Overstress
- Design error
- Excessive Load
- Dynamic Effects
- Secondary Effects

Wind Excitation
- Aeroelastic Instability
- Fatigue from wind induced oscillation
- Static wind load

External Event
- Sabotage
- Vehicle collision
- Sonic boom

Superstructure Defect

Articulation
- Chain Bent Post Slots
- Toggle Links

Trusses

Hangers

Towers
- Screw Pin Dowels at base
- Bracing Failure
- Buckling Failure

Chain Bent Post, Ohio N.

Gussett Plate U7N

Connection Box at U13N Direction of Loads?

Cleavage Fractures In Hangers 17N, 19N

Fracture L12-L13N

Pre-existent flaw?

Other Fractures

Evidence of Critical Flaws in Fractures

Direction of Loads At Fracture

Fatigue?

Evidence of "Triggers"?

Fatigue?

Paint on Fracture Surface

Erection?

Later Painting? Critical?

Eyebar Chain

Ohio Side Span?

Main Span?

W. Va. Side Span?

Joint C13N

Eyebar No. 33 Slipped Off pin?

Fracture In Eyebar No. 330

Overstress on Normal Section

Normal Stress, Pre-existent defect

Dynamic Effects Live Load?

Abnormal Loading Due to prior failure?

Actual Stress Level

Critical Stress Intensity Factor for Material At 32°F

Shock Loading Due to "trigger" fracture?

Residual Stresses Due to Heat Treatment

Stress Concentration Effects, Plastic

Mechanism of Flaw Growth

Hydrogen-Embrittlement?

Stress-Corrosion?

Fatigue?

Atmospheric Agent?

Corrosion-Fatigue?

Fretting Effects?

LOGIC FRAMEWORK FOR CONDUCT OF INVESTIGATION

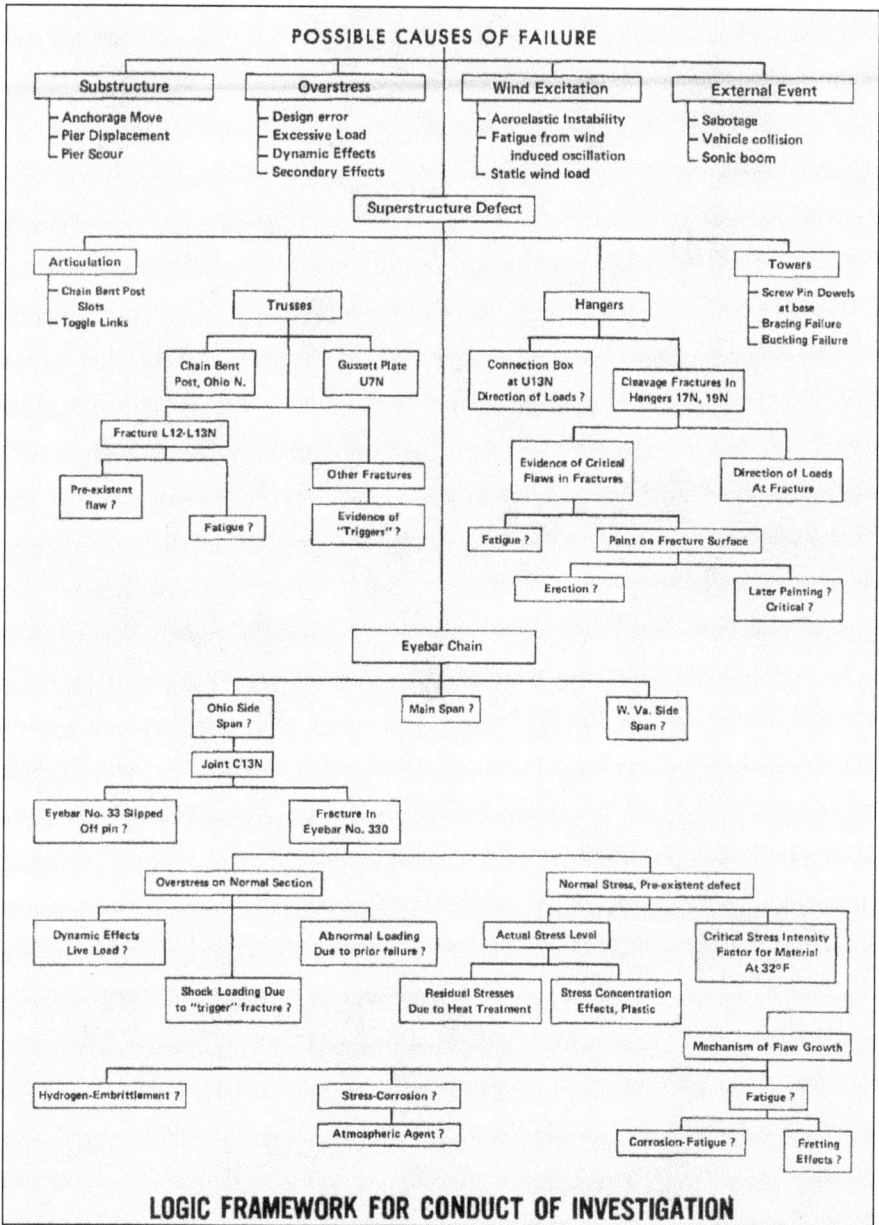

The investigation into the fall of the Silver Bridge was exceptionally thorough. This flow chart, from the National Transportation Safety Board's final report, illustrates the different lines of investigation undertaken to determine the cause of the disaster. All conceivable possibilities, even highly unlikely ones, were analyzed. One significant question was whether eyebar 330 failed because it was somehow different from the other eyebars. For example, investigators wanted to know if the steel used in eyebar 330 was inferior to that in others, or if there were any defects that caused it to break. Tests revealed that eyebar 330 was in no way different from the other eyebars. In fact, similar stress corrosion cracks were found on other eyebars that had not yet failed. It was concluded that eyebar 330 broke due to undetected stress corrosion cracks whose formation was aided by the environmental conditions present at the bridge site. (Courtesy of National Transportation Safety Board.)

Once eyebar 330 broke, a rapid sequence of events occurred that led to the catastrophic collapse of the bridge. The sudden change in forces caused eyebar 33—sister to eyebar 330 and located inside and parallel to 330—to slip off the end of the connecting pin. With both eyebars of the chain segment now released, the northern suspension chain was completely severed and the collapse of the bridge unavoidable. A contributing factor to the fall was the lack of redundancy in the suspension chains. Redundancy is a basic engineering principle whereby multiple structural elements are able to support a load if one component fails. Because only two eyebars were present in each suspension chain segment, if one eyebar failed, the bridge could easily become unstable. Here, a portion of the suspension chain and a connection joint are visible to the right of the tree at center. (Courtesy of the Gallia County Historical Genealogical Society.)

When the Silver Bridge was built, it was constructed well within the building standards of the time. Although the potential design flaws seem obvious in retrospect, they were not apparent to the designers, who thought they had built a safe and durable bridge. (Courtesy of Charles Towner.)

Two other bridges were built in a similar manner to the Silver Bridge: the Florianopolis Bridge in Brazil and the St. Mary's Bridge in West Virginia, seen here. The St. Mary's Bridge was razed in 1971. The Florianopolis Bridge still stands and is open to pedestrians. It differs from the Silver Bridge in that each segment of its suspension chain contains four eyebars. (Courtesy of the Hays family of Newport, Ohio.)

Five

THE VICTIMS

A total of 46 people lost their lives in the collapse of the Silver Bridge. Each was a treasured family member and a part of the community. Some families were utterly devastated and lost multiple members. Others lost the family breadwinner. Some lost a father or mother. Many people lost friends. The pain of these losses lingers on even 44 years after the fall of the Silver Bridge.

One of the most troubling aspects of disasters is their arbitrariness. Why this particular group of people on the bridge at the time of the collapse? Certainly, many victims were locals and used the bridge every day, but others traveled long distances to be on the bridge at that fateful time. For every person who was on the bridge, there were several who, by quirk of fate, were not. In the end, whether or not a certain person was on or off the bridge when it collapsed probably comes down to chance. This chapter stands as a tribute to all of the victims of the Silver Bridge. Although photographs were not available for every victim, those who are not pictured are not forgotten.

SPONSOR
1992
GIRLS SOFTBALL LEAGUE
Point Pleasant, West Virginia

№ 0100

SILVER ANNIVERSARY SEASON

1967 1992

DEDICATED
To the Memory of

Catherine (Cathy) Lucille Byus
Right Fielder   Shoppers Mart 1967

Born October 29, 1957
Perished December 15, 1967

On the Silver Bridge

President

Secretary

Officers

V.P.	Rick Halstead	Trustee	Jim Stearns
Treas.	Jeannie Sayre	Trustee	Fred Surbaugh
Concessions	Sue Swisher	Trustee	Rick Smith

Catherine Lucille Byus (above, first row, third from left) was 10 years old at the time of the disaster. She was riding with her mother and two-month-old sister near the center of the bridge when it collapsed. All three died. Mrs. Byus and the baby were found downriver several weeks later, becoming the 30th and 31st official bridge victims. Cathy's body was never recovered. Seen at left is a pamphlet from the 25th anniversary of the Silver Bridge tragedy. That year's softball season was dedicated to the memory of Cathy Byus. (Above, courtesy of Linda Oates; left, courtesy of PPRM.)

Donna Jean Casey, seen here with her husband and children, perished on the Silver Bridge. She worked part-time as a waitress at the Dance Restaurant in Kanauga, Ohio. At the time of the collapse, she was riding with Maxine Sturgeon and Marvin Wamsley, both of whom were also killed. (Courtesy of Linda Lane.)

Thomas Allen Cantrell worked for the Ohio Publishing Company. On December 15, his last job of the day was to take a load of newspapers to Point Pleasant. Having finished this, he was on his way back to Gallipolis when the bridge fell. This was supposed to be his last day working for Ohio Publishing; he was going to California to be a cartoonist. (Courtesy of Carol Cantrell.)

Cecil Clyde Counts, age 48, was friends with Melvin and Margaret Mae Cantrell (no relation to Thomas Cantrell) and was in their car at the time of the disaster. He had just finished chopping wood when the Cantrells asked if he would ride to town with them. When she donated this photograph, Counts's daughter Jean Counts Bush stated that she did not realize how young he looked when he died. (Courtesy of Jean Counts Bush.)

James W. Hawkins was the district manager of the Ohio area for the Firestone Tire and Rubber Company. Each year, Firestone ran a holiday promotion where they gave away Christmas albums. Hawkins had just dropped off some albums at the Point Pleasant Firestone store, which had run out, and was headed home to Ohio when the Silver Bridge fell. (Courtesy of Thayre Hawkins and Kate Hawkins Cokonougher.)

Bobby Lee Head was riding home with Ronald Sims. Head was the supervisor of production at the Goodyear plant, had served 12 years in the Navy, and was a graduate of the University of Chattanooga. His body is buried in the National Cemetery in Chattanooga, Tennessee. (Courtesy of Terri Head.)

Several families lost multiple members in the Silver Bridge disaster. One family especially hard hit was the Meadows of Point Pleasant. Father James F. Meadows (32, left) and son James Timothy "Timmy" Meadows (3, below) both died in the collapse. Their bodies were found in their car on December 18, 1967. Alma Louise Duff, who was riding with them, also perished. James Meadows had dedicated his life to the Point Pleasant Police Department. Timmy Meadows was one of several children lost in the Silver Bridge disaster and was one of the youngest victims. (Both, courtesy of Carolyn Meadows Harris.)

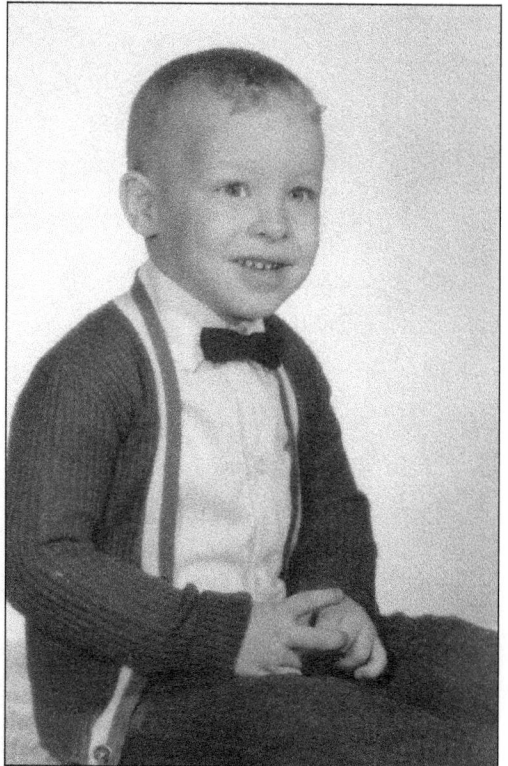

Alva "Bud" Lane (second from right) was a World War II veteran. He and Horace Donald Cremeans were on their way home from work at the Marietta Manufacturing Plant in Point Pleasant. They had almost reached the Ohio side and were directly behind the Transcon tractor-trailer when the bridge fell. (Courtesy of John Lane.)

Frederick Dean Miller, seen here with his two children, was 27 at the time of the disaster. He and Paul A. Scott were riding in the car of James Pullen near the center of the bridge. Of the three, only Scott survived. Miller is buried at the Mound Hill Cemetery in Gallipolis, Ohio. (Courtesy of Mike Miller.)

Nora Isabelle Nibert (right) worked for the Quality Manufacturing Company in Point Pleasant. She and Darius Northup (not shown) were in her Pontiac when the bridge fell. She was one of the first victims recovered. Her body was buried in Beale Chapel Cemetery in Apple Grove, West Virginia. (Courtesy of Roxie Nibert Stover and Willard Nibert.)

Leo Otto "Doc" Sanders, seen here several years before the collapse, was the driver of the Picken's Cab Company taxi. The cab company had owned this particular car for about six months, and Sanders was its only driver. The taxi had started out as cab 3, but Sanders asked if it could be changed to 13. So, it was cab 13 when the bridge fell. On the night of the collapse, a different driver was supposed to take the passenger over the bridge. However, that driver was not available, so Sanders agreed to take him. Sanders's 10-year-old son, Robert, usually rode with him, but his father did not let him go on this trip. The Sanders family lived on Ninth Street in Point Pleasant, next to the flood wall. His other son, Steven, age 16, was looking out the window and saw the bridge fall. (Courtesy of Sanders family.)

Ronald Robert Sims was a designer at the Goodyear plant. He left work late on December 15 because he had waited to give Bobby Head a ride home. He was the last victim recovered. His body was found on June 22, 1968, by two fishermen at the mouth of Crab Creek, approximately 10 miles downstream from the bridge site. (Courtesy of Kay Sims Quimby).

Memorial services were held for Ronald Sims on June 2, 1968. At the time of the ceremony, his body was still missing, which caused significant hardship for his family. Not only did it prevent them from gaining a sense of closure, but without a death certificate, the family was also not eligible for many critical services. (Courtesy of Kay Sims Quimby).

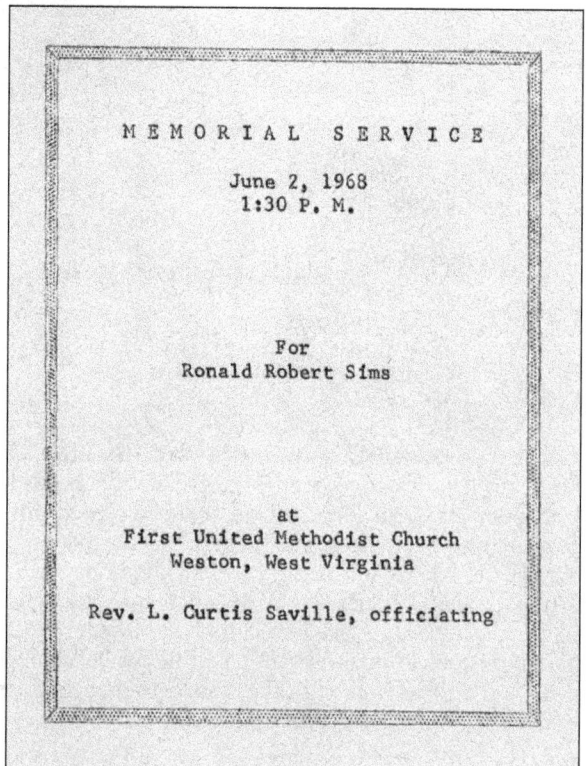

MEMORIAL SERVICE

June 2, 1968
1:30 P. M.

For
Ronald Robert Sims

at
First United Methodist Church
Weston, West Virginia

Rev. L. Curtis Saville, officiating

Charles and Oma Smith of Bidwell, Ohio, both died on the Silver Bridge. They were married on September 19, 1927, and had lived in the area for about 16 years. Charles Smith had been retired for one year from the Chesapeake & Ohio Railroad. (Courtesy of the Smith family.)

Eugene Towe was in the sleeper compartment of William Needham's Roadway truck when it sank to the bottom of the river. December 15, 1967, was supposed to be Towe's last day as a truck driver. He had purchased a farm, built a house, and was planning to start a new life as a farmer. He had a wife and three children at home. (Courtesy of Danny Towe.)

Husband and wife Paul and Lillian Wedge were both killed on the Silver Bridge. At the time of the collapse, they were near the center of the bridge traveling towards Point Pleasant. Paul Wedge was a representative for the International Brotherhood of Boilermakers and was the first president of the OhKan Coin Club. The Point Pleasant Junior-Senior High School auditorium was named in their memory. (Courtesy of Wedge family.)

James Alfred White was a beloved coach for Point Pleasant High School. Kristy Blazer Woodall remembers being at a basketball game when word came that Coach White was missing. The crowd was quiet, and the only sound in the gym was that of the basketball echoing. (Courtesy of LuAnne White Burke.)

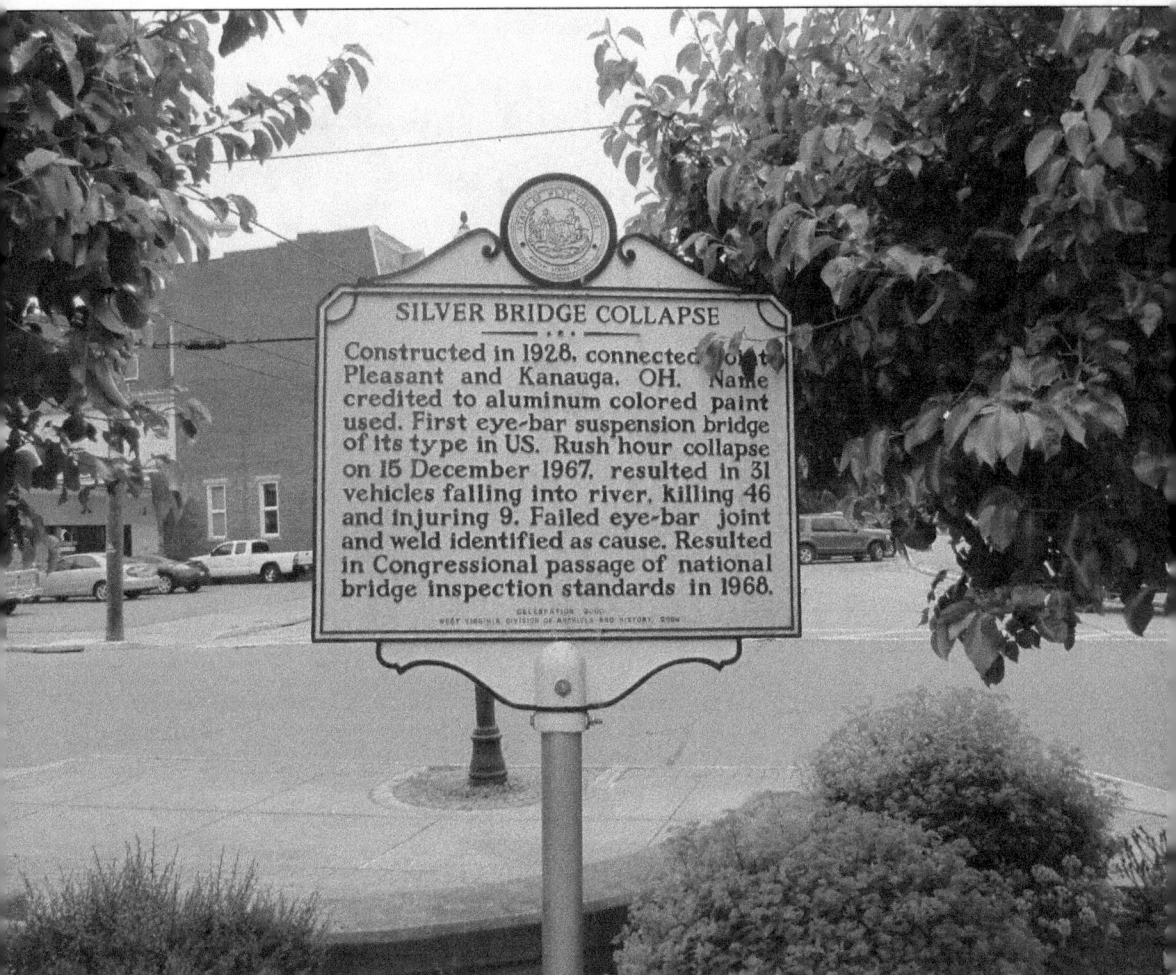

SILVER BRIDGE COLLAPSE

Constructed in 1928, connected Point Pleasant and Kanauga, OH. Name credited to aluminum colored paint used. First eye-bar suspension bridge of its type in US. Rush hour collapse on 15 December 1967, resulted in 31 vehicles falling into river, killing 46 and injuring 9. Failed eye-bar joint and weld identified as cause. Resulted in Congressional passage of national bridge inspection standards in 1968.

In 2000, a memorial was erected in Point Pleasant to the victims of the Silver Bridge disaster. It stands at the end of Sixth Street, where the West Virginia bridge approach once stood. One of two markers on the site, this West Virginia historical marker describes the disaster. (Courtesy of Stephan Bullard.)

Also at the Sixth Street site, this brickwork memorial has the name of each bridge victim inscribed on one brick. Though located at a busy intersection and adjacent to a modern parking lot, the site is typically quiet. It is a peaceful place to remember those who were lost. (Courtesy of Jim Roach family.)

Six

LEGACY OF THE SILVER BRIDGE

The fall of the Silver Bridge was the beginning of a logistical nightmare for local residents. Many people had built their lives around the bridge and, after its collapse, suddenly found themselves cut off from their work. The vital Route 35 transportation artery was also severed. In the aftermath of the disaster, it was critical to get traffic moving again and to find an efficient way to transport people across the river. The short-term solution was to run a ferry service between Ohio and West Virginia. This worked, but it was far from ideal. The main solution was to rebuild a roadway bridge as quickly as possible. In a fantastic display of motivation and engineering, a new bridge, the Silver Memorial Bridge, was dedicated exactly two years after the collapse.

Much has changed in the area since 1967. Point Pleasant and Gallipolis have continued to develop and are now home to many new residents. To these newcomers and to passing travelers, few outward signs exist of the Silver Bridge disaster. The new bridge superficially resembles the original span, but few visitors crossing the new structure probably know about the collapse that occurred a short distance to the north. Time has a way of covering old wounds, but it is important to remember the 1967 disaster and the victims and families it affected.

The collapse of the Silver Bridge was a national tragedy. As a symbol of the country's sympathy and support, Pres. Lyndon B. Johnson sent the following telegram to West Virginia governor Hulett C. Smith on December 18, 1967: "The nation has been saddened by the Silver Bridge tragedy and I express deepest sympathy to you and through you to the stricken families and the people of West Virginia and Ohio. As you know, immediately upon learning of the disaster all appropriate federal agencies were called upon to render rescue and recovery assistance coordinated by the office of emergency planning. They have been at the scene with you and will continue as long as needed. Also, in addition to conducting an investigation of the causes, we are rushing plans to help you restore transportation across the river and help you rebuild the bridge. Every possible help will continue to be rendered." (Courtesy of Gallia County Historical Genealogical Society.)

The loss of the Silver Bridge significantly disrupted traffic and commerce in the region. It was the only bridge across the Ohio River in the immediate vicinity; the closest bridges were 14 miles north at Mason, West Virginia, and 41 miles south at Huntington, West Virginia. Thus, anyone wishing to use Route 35 needed to make a significant detour to reach their destination. This not only inconvenienced drivers, but it also diverted a great deal of business from the area. In a February 7, 1968, meeting with officials from West Virginia and Ohio, Pres. Lyndon B. Johnson stressed the need to quickly rebuild a bridge at Point Pleasant. It was estimated that the loss of the Silver Bridge was costing $1 million per month in lost time and extra mileage and was causing major economic stress to the region. (Courtesy of USACE.)

Until more permanent measures could be taken, ferries were used to transport vehicles across the Ohio. Ferry service could not be started immediately, however, because a new concrete approach had to be built on the Ohio side and an existing approach had to be inspected on the West Virginia side. Around February 26, 1968, ferries began to operate between Henderson, West Virginia, and Kanauga, Ohio. Two ferries were normally in service, one that held eight cars and one that held 15 cars. Initial rates were 25¢ for pedestrians, 50¢ for cars, $3 for tractor-trailers, and $10 for trucks carrying petroleum products or explosives. The ferries helped alleviate traffic congestion but were only a stopgap measure. Actual crossing times were short, usually about five or six minutes, but long lines formed and drivers frequently had to wait for long periods before they had a chance to cross. (Courtesy of Joan and Ralph Robbins.)

Significant resources were mobilized so that a new bridge could be built as quickly as possible. The site of the replacement bridge was announced on February 23, 1968. A slight change in location had been decided upon; instead of crossing the river directly at Point Pleasant, the new bridge would be located about 1.5 miles south and would connect Henderson with Gallipolis. The design of the bridge would be different too. Gone were the elegant but flawed eyebar suspension chains. Instead, the new bridge would be a conventional cantilever design. The bridge was constructed quickly but carefully. The first concrete was poured for the Ohio approach on July 1, 1968. Overall construction took 580 days and cost $14.5 million. This photograph shows one of the new bridge piers as it nears completion. (Courtesy of George and Karen Baker.)

The new bridge, named the Silver Memorial Bridge, was much larger than the original. Although somewhat shorter—1,950 feet long compared to 2,235 feet long—it was higher, wider, and constructed with four times more steel. The new bridge needed to be robust, as it was expected to carry a great deal of traffic. When the original Silver Bridge opened in 1928, about 685 vehicles crossed it per day. By 1967, this number had jumped to 9,400. The new bridge was expected to soon carry at least 19,500 vehicles daily. To account for this heavy workload, the Silver Memorial Bridge was one of the first bridges to be built with four lanes. Here, the bridge is seen partway through construction. The two piers are finished, but the middle span has yet to be constructed. (Courtesy of George McClintock.)

The dedication of the Silver Memorial Bridge was held on December 15, 1969. Its opening fulfilled a promise made by Pres. Lyndon B. Johnson, who had pledged that a new roadway bridge would be in operation near Point Pleasant within two years of the disaster. Traffic could once again move freely through the area, and residents no longer needed to make long detours or wait for a ferry to cross the river. During the opening ceremonies, attendees were allowed to walk the bridge. Above, a chilly-looking family descends one of the new approaches. Below, several groups arrive at the West Virginia side. (Both, courtesy of George McClintock.)

Above, a setting January sun shines through the supports of the Silver Memorial Bridge in 2012. Though of a different design, the external features of the new bridge are very much like the original. By all accounts, the bridge is safe and reliable. As before, many locals cross it several times a day. It is interesting to think about how the town of Point Pleasant (below, seen from the center of the Silver Memorial Bridge) might have developed if the original Silver Bridge had remained standing, as the new bridge passes well south of the town instead of directly through it. (Both, courtesy of Stephan Bullard.)

This photograph looks toward the remains of the Silver Bridge's West Virginia approach from Sixth Street in Point Pleasant. It was taken at 4:50 p.m. on December 15, 1968, one year—almost to the minute—after the bridge collapsed. A note on the back of the photograph states, "It was not dark and the weather was nearly the same." The first part is a reference to the commonly held belief that the bridge fell in darkness. Sunset on December 15 was approximately 5:07 p.m., so this was in fact not the case. However, night arrived very soon after the fall, and many people first heard about it or arrived at the scene after dark. Given the similar conditions, this is almost exactly what someone would have seen as they approached the bridge on the evening of the collapse. (Courtesy of George McClintock.)

The West Virginia bridge approach remained standing long after the disaster. Here, vehicles have been placed across the bottom to prevent curious onlookers from walking up the ramp. It was not until December 9, 1968, that the city council recommended its removal. The approach was dismantled, and the grounds were given to the city. About the same time, Ohio officially also decided to remove the Ohio approach and bridge piers. (Courtesy of Wanda O'Dell.)

This photograph of the West Virginia bridge approach (in the distance) was taken soon after the collapse. The mailbox at right marks the location of the Mason County Insurance Company. Coauthor Ruth Fout was working here in 1967 when the bridge fell. (Courtesy of Wanda O'Dell.)

This 2012 photograph shows the bottomland where the Ohio-side bridge approach stood. The bridge crossed the riverbank approximately in the center, near where the clump of large trees now grows. The area remains undeveloped, and few reminders exist to mark the presence of the Silver Bridge. (Courtesy of Stephan Bullard.)

On the West Virginia side, a parking lot and fully sealed flood wall now stand where the bridge ramp began. The three trees in the center frame the Silver Bridge sidewalk memorial, and the Silver Bridge historical marker is just visible between the left two trees. In the left foreground is an older historical marker about Ohio. (Courtesy of Stephan Bullard.)

The impacts of disasters linger on long after the visible signs of the tragedy have vanished. As long as victims or their loved ones remain alive, the effects of a disaster continue to reverberate. The collapse of the Silver Bridge remains a touchstone event for the small communities along the Ohio River. Nearly every longtime resident has a story about where they were when they heard about it or how it affected them. Even 44 years later, the communities continue to bear the scars of the disaster. Those who lost families and friends continue to suffer their loss. A final memorial stands on the West Virginia bank of the river, beyond the flood wall, where the Silver Bridge once stood. The plaque reads, "Site of the Silver Bridge, Collapsed December 15, 1967, 46 Lives Lost." (Courtesy of Stephan Bullard.)

Adler, E. Albert Jr. "Bert"
Bennett, Julius Oliver "J.O."
Blackman, Leo H.
Boggs, Marjorie S.
Boggs, Kristye Ann
Byus, Hilda Gertrude
Byus, Kimberly Lynn
Byus, Catherine Lucille "Cathy"
Casey, Donna Jean
Cantrell, Melvin Aaron
Cantrell, Thomas Allen
Counts, Cecil Clyde
Cremeans, Horace "Donald"
Cundiff, Harold D.
Darst, Alonzo "Lonnie"
Duff, Alma L.
Hawkins, James W.
Head, Bobby Lee
Higley, Forrest Raymond
Lane, Alva Bernard "Bud"
Lee, Thomas Howard "Bus"
Mabe, Gene Harold
Maxwell, James Richard
Mayes, Darlene K.
McManus, Gerald
Meadows, James F.
Meadows, James Timothy "Timmy"
Miller, Frederick "Dean"
Moore, Ronnie Gene
Nibert, Nora Isabelle
Northup, Darius E.
Pullen, James Otto
Sanders, Leo Otto "Doc"
Sims, Ronald R.
Smith, Charles Thomas
Smith, Oma Letha
Sturgeon, Maxine Ellen
Taylor, Denzil
Taylor, Glenna Mae
Towe, Robert Eugene
Turner, Victor William "Vic"
Turner, Mrs. William Victor "Maxine"
Wamsley, Marvin L.
Wedge, Paul D.
Wedge, Lillian Eleanor Herrig
White, James Alfred

BIBLIOGRAPHY

After-Action Report, Silver Bridge Collapse, Point Pleasant, W. Va. 15 December 1967.
    Huntington, WV: U.S. Army Engineers Huntington District, Corps of Engineers,
    Department of the Army, March 1968.

Akesson, Björn. *Understanding Bridge Collapses.* London: Taylor and Francis Group, 2008.

Armagnac, Alden P. "Our Worst Bridge Disaster: Why Did It Happen?" *Popular Science.* No.
    192, March 1968.

Bennett, J.A. and Harold Mindlin. "Metallurgical Aspects of the Failure of the Point Pleasant
    Bridge." *Journal of Testing and Evaluation* 1 (March 1973): 152–161.

Canfield, John A. *State Papers and Public Addresses of Hulett C. Smith, Twenty-Seventh
    Governor of West Virginia, 1965–1969.* Charleston, WV: 1969.

"Collapse of I-35W Highway Bridge, Minneapolis, Minnesota, August 1, 2007." *Highway
    Accident Report NTSB/HAR-08/03* Washington, DC: National Transportation Safety Board,
    2008.

"Collapse of US 35 Highway Bridge, Point Pleasant, West Virginia, December 15, 1967."
    Highway Accident Report NTSB-HAR-71-1 Washington, DC: National Transportation Safety
    Board, 1970.

Lichtenstein, Abba G. "The Silver Bridge Collapse Recounted." *Journal of Performance of
    Constructed Facilities* 7 (November 1993): 249–261.

"Point Pleasant Bridge Collapse." *National Bureau of Standards Technical News Bulletin* 55
    (August 1971): 196–197.

Woodall, Kristy B. *The Silver Bridge Disaster: The Way We Remember It.* Point Pleasant, WV:
    self-published, 1994.

Visit us at
arcadiapublishing.com

www.ingramcontent.com/pod-product-compliance
Lightning Source LLC
Chambersburg PA
CBHW050554110426
42813CB00008B/2351